D0233501

HAYDEN ROBERTS is in the Faculty of Extension, University of Alberta.

Community development is often shaped by purely economic and political considerations, but it can also function as a process of education that expresses the perceptions of people and enhances their control of their society.

Drawing on his experience of economic models of development in Africa and Canada, Hayden Roberts designs a practice theory of development that emerges from, and responds to, the needs of the community itself. His analysis emphasizes the political nature of the process and the central role of adult education in achieving the goals of a given community. His theory, in brief, is that affected people are more capable than outsiders of perceiving and assessing the conditions of their lives, and that, with appropriate inspiration and guidance, they can plan and act to change these conditions for the better.

Theories of learning, communication, intergroup and interpersonal behaviour, organization, economic development, and political change are all utilized towards the formulation of a comprehensive theory and practical approach to community development planning. Roberts advances a people-oriented approach to development that draws its models from various disciplines and takes into account the local social, economic, and material needs of the community as well as the native abilities of the people concerned. His conclusions are equally relevant to third world societies and to minority groups or sub-cultures in industrialized societies, and they are presented with remarkable clarity and conciseness. He sifts through a maze of theories and emerges with a plausible theory of community development that is backed at every stage by the lessons of practical experience.

This broadly based and humane work will interest all concerned with the process of community development, from planning to action.

HAYDEN ROBERTS

Community Development: learning and action

UNIVERSITY OF TORONTO PRESS

Toronto   Buffalo   London

© University of Toronto Press 1979
Toronto Buffalo London
Reprinted 1982
Printed in Canada

ISBN 0-8020-3437-4 (cloth)
ISBN 0-8020-6351-9 (paper)

Library of Congress Cataloging in Publication Data

Roberts, Hayden, 1922 –
  Community development.

  Bibliography: p.
  Includes index.
  ISBN 0-8020-5437-4   ISBN 0-8020-6351-9 pbk.
  1. Underdevelopment areas. 2. Community
  development. 3. Adult education. I. Title.
  HN980.R6   309.2'6   78-12986

301.15
ROB

Contents

vi Contents

Figures

Preface

A personal belief about the nature of man and of the proper way in which the development of individuals and of society should be ordered seems to be implicit in the outlook and observable behaviour of those who work and/or teach in the field of community development. I wish at the outset to indicate the viewpoint which I bring to a discussion of the subject.

My own view of the term 'development,' and particularly 'community development,' has taken shape in the circumstances through which I have come to work in this field. An early step along the way was prompted by a dissatisfaction with the emphasis placed on economic, as opposed to political, development in Rhodesia, and in the Federation of Rhodesia and Nyasaland while it existed (between 1953 and 1963). As I saw it, as an official involved in economic administration, it was a matter of concentrating on economic development, and on those types of economic investment which promised the highest annual increments to the gross national product and to the profits of external investors, with very little real regard for how the national product was to be distributed among the total population, black and white. Economic development under the control of minority governments was glorified as the way to a better life, the enjoyment of which would show to the Africans the irrelevance – even the distraction – of political aspirations.

This emphasis on economic development was not peculiar to policy-makers in that part of central Africa at that time – the 1950s. For instance, at the time of the first World Bank loan to Southern Rhodesia in 1952, for electric power installations, it was not part of the World Bank's thinking that investment in such non-material activities as education was economically justified. Ten years later the World Bank had changed its policy to include education as being worthy of its investment, though still within

the economic mode of developing people as human capital, but the underlying intentions of the Rhodesian policy-makers were still to concentrate
development in the economic sphere while narrowing both the benefits
of such developments and the possibilities of participation of the black
majority in the process of political decision-making.

It was in such a situation that my perception of development as being
governed by political power began to be formed. The emphasis in development policies and practices, and the direction which development
took, depended on who were able to make political decisions and on their
values and view of the world, in other words, on the paradigm within
which they operated. Economic development, that is, an emphasis on the
exploitation and development of natural resources and the shaping of
people's lives by patterns of production and consumption which fitted the
needs of those who were able to make decisions, was the central element
in the paradigm.

More basically, I suppose, I had come to distrust the assumptions of
classical Adam Smithian economic studies, that every individual, in pursuing his own ends, helps society the most. Too many structures and special interests had built up, creating *imperfect* competition. (Other things
never are equal.) The most important of these were the special interests
of the developed, industrialized powers and the whole structure of international trade exemplified in the core-periphery model of economic development. The core was the metropolitan, industrialized western world,
in whose service and for whose benefit the periphery – the developing
countries – existed; in other words, colonialism. And though Marx himself appeared to start from a different – and to me more acceptable – view
of society, I found myself not much more comfortable with Marxian economics as a basic framework for human affairs, because of its analysis of
such affairs in materialistic terms.

I found myself increasingly in sympathy with the expression of feelings, and the seeking for the roots of their tradition, of Africans who were
coming to an awareness of other values which were not spoken to by
material development. The same expressions are now being voiced in the
Canadian north by the Indians, Métis (halfbreed), and Inuit people in
response to the same colonialist/capitalist assumptions of southern Cana-
dians, and the urge on the part of the latter to see development simply in
economic terms.

Such a distrust – or at least a questioning – now appears to be shown in
a growing consciousness among some economists of a certain lack of ele-
gance in measurements of satisfaction based purely on short-term market

gains in the form of maximum profits (Bernthal 1968; Davis 1971,428-36) and in the behavioural theory of economic enterprises which introduces into economic decision-making the possibility of beneficial, if somewhat accidental, social consequences both inside and outside the enterprise, e.g. 'public services are provided in excess of those required' (Cohen and Cyert 1965,333). From other directions there appear propositions that economic impetus even comes after, and results from, non-economic factors: for example, McClelland's (1961) view that an achievement motive lies behind economic drive; Hagan's (1964) view that creativeness is, so to speak, pre-economic; Weber's older contention that the capitalist drive comes from a certain religious orientation (Tawney 1938); and Taylor's view that it is the anal, as distinct from the oral, personality which engenders economic as well as social change (McLeish 1969,34-5).

On the other hand, I do not discount the benefits of material progress to people living at or below a subsistence level. It is insensitive to try to induce 'higher' motives – in Maslow's terms – in people whose basic physiological and material needs are not being met.

My next step toward an active interest in community development was by way of adult education, again in Rhodesia. I came new to such an occupation after some years of work as a government servant engaged in the remoteness of economic and financial planning, and, for a period, in the absurdities of diplomatic life, and I was now groping my way into a closer involvement with people faced with bewildering change. I shared their bewilderment in the sense that I had to perceive the world anew. In such an environment adult education has much to do with helping people to gain not only knowledge, but also skills with which to organize their lives to cope with problems of urbanization, industrialization, small business operations, co-operation, etc. So adult education – in fact, education at all levels – becomes part of the process by which people's lives are made more satisfying, or at any rate less distressing. The kind of adult education in which I found myself increasingly involved was working with groups of people who wished to come to grips with, and have an effect on, their living conditions, through increased political awareness and power.

My experience in the practice of adult education, and my perception that such education had a political purpose, was reinforced by study of the history of adult education in Britain. There was a continuing tension in nineteenth-century England between, on the one hand well-intentioned humanitarians such as Maurice and Toynbee, and the limited objectives of the Mechanics Institutes, and on the other hand the aspirations of unskilled workers who adopted the slogan, 'Knowledge is power' (Kelly 1970; Harrison 1961). This tension led to the formation of Working Men's Colleges and Institutes, and gave rise to the involvement of trade unions, co-operatives, and eventually the Labour party, in forms of adult education designed to prepare people for participation in the political life of the country. The subsequent history of adult education in Britain indicates that such politically-oriented learning has not been entirely acceptable to influential elements in the field. The neutral Workers Education Association was opposed by newly-formed and more militant Labour Colleges, which in 1921 formed the National Council of Labour Colleges, and had a clear political orientation. In more recent years there has been a revival of interest in Britain in adult education explicitly aimed at increasing the ability of working class people to 'name their world,' and take a part in shaping it (Freire 1972,76). Lovatt describes recent conscious efforts in Liverpool to create a functional relationship between adult education and community development among working class people (Lovatt 1975).

In adult education there is a continuing tension – which too seldom comes to the surface – between the conservative (and in *practice* the dominant) view that adult education is simply more of the usual, i.e., expanded opportunities for fitting oneself, with some creativity and minimum stress, into the existing socio-economic scheme of things, and the more radical view that adult education is an examination, and where appropriate, a rejection of the conventional wisdom. I find myself on the latter side, and from this perspective I see a natural merging of adult education and community development.

This merging is especially apparent in the sharpening in recent years of the focus on non-formal adult education, as distinct from formal and informal education (Coombs *et al.* 1973). Formal education is that which takes place within the institutions of learning such as schools and universities, and informal education is the lifelong process whereby people acquire attitudes, values, skills, and knowledge from daily experience in their environment. Non-formal education embraces organized learning outside the formal system, e.g., farm training, family planning education, village leadership training, and Ahmed and Coombs (1975) reveal the wide range of such development – oriented education in a number of countries in South America, Africa, and Asia. At the same time, many of the sources of informal education, such as radio, newspapers, and libraries, are important investments in community development.

The desire to have more control over the forces which shape one's life is not peculiar to black people in Rhodesia and working class people in Britain. It appears in western Canadian society, not only among the native people, Indian and Métis, who see themselves in many respects in the same position as that in which Rhodesian blacks see themselves, but also among relatively 'liberated' people – more or less prosperous suburban and urban groups. I come to this conclusion through having worked with a number of groups in Alberta, including the Junior League, the National Council of Jewish Women, and church groups of different denominations. One difference between more prosperous groups and poorer ones lies in the degree to which they perceive the controlling forces to lie outside themselves and their group, or within themselves and their group; the more prosperous, middle-class ones start with a higher feeling of confidence in their own power to influence change.

What follows in this book is, therefore, an analysis of community development from two perspectives, combining an educational model in which the emphasis is on learning, and a political model. I do not say that there are not other perspectives from which development may be viewed. The economic model, in particular, is one which has been widely followed in Africa and in parts of Canada and elsewhere. As I have said, economic well-being cannot be disdained, and in chapter 3 I refer to the communication model as it relates to the linkage between a community and its environment.

In recent years, in both 'developed' and 'developing' countries, there has been a growing interest in the need to activate people, to the end that there should be wider popular participation in this political process. The interest has expressed itself in such terms as 'community development,' 'social animation,' 'social development,' and 'citizen participation,' and has manifested itself in the engagement by governments at all levels – national, provincial, and municipal – of workers with titles such as community development officer, community relations officer, and community services co-ordinator. In many cases, such as in the American Model Cities programs, these workers were employed to serve the interests of the employing agencies rather than to facilitate real participation by the people. So, as a sort of countervailing force to institutional government – even a movement of subversion – groups and associations whose purpose is to influence governments and improve social conditions are now engaging such workers to act as animators and trainers. Some examples of this kind of effort are the Canadian Native Brotherhood, the Indian Association of Alberta, churches and church groups, Black caucuses in the USA, and associations of West Indians and of Pakistanis in Britain. There are other institutions, such as universities and local education authorities, which are engaging members of their staff in a variety of community services, and there are increasing numbers of private organizations acting as consultants in this field.

Those already working in the field come from a variety of educational backgrounds and disciplines. Many have trained as social workers, others in such fields as engineering, agriculture, science, sociology, while others have had a liberal arts education. Still others do not have a formal training or higher education. In the course of their work most of them engage in a process of continuing education on the job, a part of which is the study of conceptual models related to community development. Some, after periods of field experience, return to university for post-graduate and/or post-experience studies.

Besides those already in the field, there is an increasing number of people studying in universities and colleges with the intention of going into community work of some sort. Since 1966, when W.W. and L.J. Biddle listed thirty-two American and Canadian universities where community development could be studied, with others 'edging over toward community development' (Biddle and Biddle 1966,286), there has been a considerable increase in the number of such programs in North America, in Europe, and in the developing countries. Moreover, since community development has to do with such notions as authority, power, leadership, human relationships, and social change, it is of interest to, and draws on the studies of those whose main work is in sociology, social psychology, geography, political science, and education. Community development is an application of such disciplines.

The idea of writing this book has grown out of my own groping for models and guides, and then from the experience of working with students of community development in three countries: Rhodesia (while it was still known as Southern Rhodesia), Scotland, and Canada. Some of the latter have, from time to time, questioned the usefulness of concepts and have wanted to get on with learning or perfecting skills – though they are often not sure what that means. One of my main purposes is to indicate that the two are not to be so simply distinguished, and that skills are used within a framework of assumptions and concepts, and with benefit of models which come out of experience, research, and reflection.

There is a view that there is no theory of community development, but a wide variety of theories from other fields which have a bearing on community development; theories of learning, communication, interpersonal and intergroup behaviour, economic development, political change, etc. Such theories rest on, and vary with, different views of life, of human nature, and of the part people take in determining the direction and manner of their living. What distinguishes community development as an *activity* is that it rests on certain underlying propositions: that people are capable of both perceiving and judging the condition of their lives; that they have the will and capacity to plan together in accordance with these judgments to change that condition for the better; that they can act together in accordance with these plans; and that such a process can be seen in terms of certain values. What distinguishes community development as a *field of study* is that the student seeks to understand processes of growth, learning, and human interaction, and social, economic, and political forms, and the extent to which these are consistent with those underlying propositions and can be applied to that continuing activity.

So, since community development is a matter of experience and skills on the one hand, and of philosophy and concepts on the other, there seems to be a need for the sort of continuing study through research and concentration which a university can provide.

This book has two principal and interlinking themes. One, which is treated more extensively, is that for the most part collectivities of people and their leaders who make up communities, find it difficult to act without having formulated or adopted some way of organizing their perceptions of, and their action in, the world around them – that is, some concept, or model – and that there are certain identifiable models which are appropriate for the kinds of action which we call community development. The other theme is that the concepts of 'community' and 'community development' need re-examination in the light of changes in communications techniques, the conditions of mass society, and observations of when and how people actually manifest collective energy.

Accordingly, the book is in three parts. The introduction (chapter 1) examines what the models are, why they are useful, and how they should be used. The following two chapters, forming part one, set the scene as far as community development is concerned. Chapter 2 examines the meaning of the terms 'community' and 'development' in the light of the changes referred to above. The definition of 'community,' in breaking away from more traditional definitions by suggesting a more explicit, discrete grouping of people, leads into the following chapter which uses social science and communication models to explain the inevitable linking of explicit, discrete groups back into broader social systems. In chapter 2, I also develop a model of the community development process, and the chapters in part two of the book take up the process and discuss a number of models in relation to the main stages of the process. The final chapter summarizes the discussion and relates it back to the two principal themes.

Acknowledgments

I wish to acknowledge the contribution which many people, in many places, have made to my learning, which I have tried to articulate in this book. They are community leaders, government servants, concerned citizens, teachers, students in Africa, Europe, and North America.

In the writing of this book I have enjoyed and benefitted particularly from the advice of Robert Atkins, Glen Eyford, Michael Kirkhorn, Gordon McIntosh, and Nola Symor. Nola Symor has been especially helpful in giving more detailed editorial comment with a view to publication.

This book has been published with the help of a grant from the Social Science Federation of Canada, using funds provided by the Social Sciences and Humanities Research Council of Canada, and a grant to the University of Toronto Press from the Andrew W. Mellon Foundation.

HAYDEN ROBERTS
Edmonton

COMMUNITY DEVELOPMENT

1

Introduction: the usefulness of models

It has been suggested in the Preface that the art and skills of community development are practised with benefit of experience, research and reflection, and that there seems to be a place for universities in providing both exposure to concepts which have come out of such research and reflection, and practice in the conceptualization of one's own experience. There are differing views about this. On the one hand there is the view that the study of community development is not 'college level education or research,' that it is not education or research at any level, but is a social reform movement (Peterson 1960,114). On the other hand, it is the view of some that to require that community development workers should learn their job by going and working in a community raises the risk of their learning at the community's expense.

What seems reasonable to propose is that community development is among those social and political activities whose principles and practices can appropriately be studied in a variety of places and situations. Some qualities important in community development are often studied and learned better outside the university than in it: a sensitivity to one's own limitations and strength at a time of crisis; the pace of decision-making and action in social life; a tolerance of ambiguity; how to handle frustration and to help others handle it; patience; passion. It is not to the university that one comes to learn such qualities as these. Most of them can be learned by experience, on the job, and in one's daily relationships. Certain organizational skills, of leadership, communication, and administration are learned in a variety of experiences and institutions outside universities. Others, such as the practical significance of theories of development and active methods of social organization and evaluation, are learned at university. In other words, different aspects of community development work can, and should, be prepared for in different ways.

I make a further assumption, which is that there is a legitimate place and role for community development workers. Many of them seem to see it in a mystical, humanistic way, more spiritual than practical, and a great deal of woolly thinking and aimless practice abounds in the field. But this is precisely why the preparation of community development workers needs to be rigorous, and why the universities' contribution to such preparation has to have intellectual sinew as well as affective content. There is a role for such a person as a social animator, or community worker, or what Alinsky frankly calls an organizer (Alinsky 1972), who can be a source of knowledge, skill, inspiration, and advice to people involved in the community development process, but the requirements of that role need to be thought out clearly in any training for such work.

ROLE OF COMMUNITY DEVELOPMENT WORKERS

One requirement is therefore to define the role of community development workers. This role is a function of being available to a group of people who, out of some dissatisfaction with their condition, wish to change that condition, and this is done by providing encouragement, advice, help, and initially leadership, as these are required.

To express the role in terms of the typology of power suggested by French and Raven, community development workers will enjoy no *reward* power; i.e., the power to reward members of the group; no *coercive* power, i.e., the perceived power to force them, by sanctions, to act in certain ways; no *legitimate* power, i.e., power which is seen as being bestowed on them because of their position in the organizational structure of the group. Their influence will derive from whatever *expert* power they have, i.e., the way they show that they have some useful expertise to offer; and possibly from *referent* power, i.e., the extent to which they become the sort of persons that members of the group would like to be (French and Raven 1959,150-67).

There is a border area between community development and political action, which raises the possibility in real life of a community development worker being drawn into the identity of the group by the members of the group. When this change of roles begins to happen it poses for the worker the same question of choice that lies between being an educator and an activist. If he makes such a choice he is moving from what is conventionally seen as the role of a community development worker to that of a more permanent leader in a group which is adopting a more formal organization, and he has to be prepared to face responsibilities which come with exercising reward, coercive, or legitimate power. He has to accept that instead of working himself out of a job in the emerging community, as it becomes capable of independent action, he is entering into a more committed type of leadership and possibly increasing the group's dependence on him. Instead of acting in an educational role, he continues to engage in acts of leadership such as convening meetings, organizing committees, and finding resources. It is a legitimate choice for any community development worker to make *as an individual*, so long as he recognizes the different role in which it will place him, what different attitudes and skills will be called into play, and the likely effect on the group.

The conventional and more commonly held view of the role of community development worker is that his influence arises mainly from expert power. If the role of the community development worker is to provide encouragement, advice, and help, one can assume that these should be in the direction of improving the group's knowledge and skill and of inducing attitudes appropriate to the situation. An important thing to remember in this connection is a point made by Homans (1950,16): 'You may become a man who is sensitive and intuitive about people and yet incapable of communicating any but your most obvious intuitions.' A community development worker has to be capable of communicating his intuitions, and the knowledge and skills he has acquired, to others.

Community development has to do with conditions of social instability and change, and it is a process of adapting to, and, as far as possible, exercising some control over such conditions. In analyzing these conditions in the contemporary world, and seeking strategies of response and control, Schon suggests that it is becoming increasingly important that this process of learning be emphasized in group behaviour. New roles of intervention become necessary – roles 'related to the responsiveness to new information (prophet, artist, visionary) and the network roles essential to design, development and management of the shifting networks on which functional systems depend' (Schon 1971,186). In one sense, community development can be seen as a set of such roles – a learning system – and the community development worker as a person modelling such roles. Schon further suggests that strategies of change should be related to and focused not on products or institutions but on purposes and functions.

A matter which arises commonly whenever two or more community development workers are gathered together is the controversy about the role of generalist and of specialist. The generalist is seen as one who is trained in a number of fields such as organization, administration, communication, and human relations, while the specialist is seen as one who has concentrated on a special field, particularly of a technical or technological nature, such as agronomy, civil engineering, or urban planning. This controversy arises in developing rural societies in disputes between agricultural extension officers and community development officers where the former claim that what is needed is solid training in the best scientific methods of increasing agricultural production, while the latter claim that what is needed is the ability to communicate, empathize, and encourage group problem-solving and decision-making. The caricature of each, as it is held by the other, is of the former as being 'hard,' directive, authoritarian, and ignorant of the nuances of human motivation, and the latter as being 'soft,' indeterminate, and incapable of giving a clear lead in any activity that leads to concrete results. Instances do exist of developing schemes in which the caricature comes near to describing the real thing: on the one hand, livestock control schemes initiated by animal husbandry experts in central Africa in ignorance of tribal attitudes toward cattle-owning, or urban renewal schemes in London or Edinburgh designed by architects and planners, consisting of hygienic high-rise apartment blocks which have no regard for the need for social contact; on the other hand, the sort of examples that Erasmus gives of evangelical but ineffective 'missionaries' in Latin America (Erasmus 1968).

At the level where each side searches out and holds up examples of the idiocy of the other, the controversy is irresolvable. What seems to be more fruitful is to discuss what knowledge, skills, and attitudes appear to be particularly appropriate in a process in which a group of people with certain problems in a changing situation undergo a process of learning to understand those problems, to formulate a set of objectives which will move them away from those problems, and then to help them to decide and to undertake certain actions to achieve these objectives.

LEARNING FOR COMMUNITY DEVELOPMENT WORK

The question is: what knowledge, skills, and attitudes are needed by a community development worker to cope with the problems and opportunities which will confront him. The discussion in chapter 2 will suggest that members of a community need to acquire *knowledge* of themselves, of the group they are in, and of their environment; *skills* – of communication and decision-making; and *attitudes* – toward people inside and outside the group. This is in the early stages of the process when the people are turning feelings to tension, unease, and frustration into a set of objectives by which they can overcome that condition. Then at the stage of turning their objectives into action, more learning begins: skills of planning, organization, and administration. And finally, there are the skills of evaluation: i.e., judging how successful any course of action is.

If these are the kinds of learning which the people themselves need in order to get the process going, it is reasonable to suggest that they are the kinds of learning appropriate for community development workers. And the latter need, in addition, to be facilitators in the learning of others.

These questions give rise to the kind of discussion in relation to learning and community development that Kaplan follows in distinguishing between logic-in-use and reconstruction of logic (Kaplan 1964,16). Logic-in-use is the intuitive process of pursuing and understanding the truth. Reconstructions of logic are rational formulations of that process – models or conceptions of what the process is. Similarly, art-in-use is the intuitive process of behaving in such a way as to create new forms and new relationships perceivable through people's senses, while reconstructions of art are formulations of that process: aesthetics, or the philosophy of art. One can use that analogy to suggest what may not be a very elegant word-image, but is not a totally inelegant concept, 'community development-in-use.' And one may distinguish between this and reconstructions of community development.

In other words, there is a set of behaviours which one could call the art of community development – what men actually do which inspires, guides, leads, persuades others to face their tensions, to learn about their social predicament, to discover ways out of it, and to act on that discovery. There are men and women who are artists in the sense of carrying out these behaviours intuitively. It is not a case of having to learn these ways of behaving, in whatever place or from whatever source; it is a case of acting intuitively. This would be community development-in-use. There are, it seems, some people in the world who have developed that art more than most of us have. One whom I have personally observed to have it is Guy Clutton-Brock of St Faith's Mission and Cold Comfort Farm in Rhodesia – until he was deported by the Smith regime (Clutton-Brock 1972; and see p. 129 below). Saul Alinsky describes how, in his early years of community organizing in Chicago, he made many moves almost intuitively, doing things 'because that was the thing to do' (Alinsky 1972,169). And there are thousands of unknown and unassuming people in many places doing the same.

Most of us, however, have to rely on a less direct process of understanding. The intuitive act of the artist, once it is done, ceases to be an intuition; it becomes a model, a symbolic representation in words, letters, numbers, paint, stone, of the product of the intuitive act. And once the artist begins to describe the process by which the product came forth, he ceases to act as an artist and begins to act as an explainer or a reconstructor. The original, intuitive symbol is something only its creator can work with; the model can be worked with by others. And insofar as a person cannot himself act intuitively in appropriate ways, or have intuitive understanding of a situation, he relies for an understanding of what to do in that situation on some model, or prescription for action (Homans 1950,17).

But even the model cannot be adopted unchanged by others; it has to be fitted by them to their own comprehension and skills. They may adapt it to their style of operating, which is, in a way, another kind of art, an ability to use the model in a personal way, even for different purposes from those for which it was created.

Kaplan goes on to suggest that intuition produces logic-in-use different from available reconstructions, but is capable of being more and more closely approximated by better reconstructions. And one can extend the analogy in community development. An intuitively correct understanding of a community development process, or of something which needs to be done as part of that process at a particular time, may enable some 'artists' to act directly in the appropriate way, without having to resort to a model or theory based on other people's experience. For other people, for whom intuition is a less developed mode of perception (Mogar 1969), models based on other people's experience are a means of understanding and of consequent action. And it is not impossible that such models may be constructed out of the experience of the intuitive actor, by an observer of that experience and of that actor's responses. As Kaplan says, 'invention can be cultivated' (Kaplan 1964,16). It is possible, through a process of learning, to enhance a skill in constructing models, and even more so is it possible to enhance a skill in recognizing appropriate models which have been created by others.

When we consider the part that universities may play in the preparation of persons to work in community development, we should be concerned not so much with the teaching of subjects as such, but with the disciplines on which they are based – disciplines in the sense of reconstructions of systems of thought which allow us to approach the art. So the thing is not simply to list subjects such as sociology, social psychology, psychology, geography, and organization theory. For instance, it is not enough to say that when we are concerned to understand the environment we turn to geography, that when we are concerned to understand social groups, we turn to sociology, when we are concerned to understand ourselves, we turn to psychology. The question is: what process of thought is it which, in pursuing these subjects, enabled us to understand? How, in all the multitude of perceptions that bombard our senses from our environment, do we bring any order to it all and begin to see it clearly enough to be able to go about our business? And more important for community development, which is a matter of very practical behaviour in the everyday world, what is it in all this study which can help the learner to behave more effectively in that world? In fact, the reality of the typical university regime does not achieve the ideal which is implicit in these questions. The kind of order into which perceived phenomena are placed, i.e., the way information is received, organized, and presented, is not governed in universities with quite that independence from outside pressures and influences which is claimed as distinguishing universities from other institutions in society.

CONCEPTUAL MODELS

Such a practical man of action as Saul Alinsky asserts that 'a way of life means a certain degree of order where things have some relationship and can be pieced together into a system that at least provides some clues to what life is about. Men have always yearned for and sought for direction by setting up religions, inventing political philosophies, creating scientific systems like Newton's, or formulating ideologies of various kinds. This is what is behind the common cliché "getting it all together"' (Alinsky 1972,xv). And these philosophies, systems, ideologies, etc. are what it is all about.

A common view of concepts is that they are statements or formulations of theory, somewhat removed from the practical business of living, and pursued in academic discussions. As Alinsky indicates, a more exact view is in the opposite direction. Abraham Kaplan (1964,46) says, with admirable clarity, that a concept is 'a rule of judging or acting, a prescription for organizing the materials of experience so as to be able to go on about our business.' As such, they appear to answer the question about what it is that helps us bring order to perceived phenomena, and discipline to our thinking. They do not simply mirror reality, thus taking away that very reality, but they perform a service in our dealings with reality (Kaplan 1964,83).

To refer back to the earlier discussion of the difference between logic-in-use and reconstructed logic, and community development-in-use and reconstructions of community development, reconstructions are models, symbolic representations of situations and behaviour. They consist of ideas, more or less clearly formulated, about (i) human beings in collectivities, (ii) aspects of behaviour, and (iii) the ways these aspects fit together and affect one another (Riley 1963,15). They allow, or help, us to understand these social phenomena and to act in relation to them. So conceptual models are organizing images of perceived phenomena, but they are more than that: Riley suggests that they are *working* models, tentative ways of construing a particular set of social phenomena and devices for guiding the formulation and solution of problems.

The model of the community development process set out in chapter 2 suggests a number of stages in that process, the first of which is the stage of getting to know and understand the problem that is causing the tensions which the group seeks to relieve. What happens at this stage is the working out, ordering, and refining of a mass of information about these tensions and making sense of it all; in other words, a process of analysis. Without the guidance of past experience in setting about such a process, it can be a long, confusing and frequently fruitless one. And in reality none of us goes through this in an experiential vacuum: 'no observations or diagnoses are ever made on 'raw facts,' because facts are really observations made within a set of concepts' (Chin 1964,201). The use of experience on the part of a practitioner means the use of experience or observation of past cases, and the trick is to choose those experiences which are relevant to current experience, in other words, to use those conceptual models which are appropriate.

Models used for this purpose of understanding a current experience or an existing situation are called analytical or structural models. Analytical science picks out some of the elements at work in particular situations and seeks to describe the relationship between them, and by cutting out some of these elements it seeks to achieve a systematic description, i.e., a certain set of relationships between certain elements. These elements and relationships will be identified within a pattern of thinking, and in terms of certain objectives. In other words, immediately we start cutting out elements in any situation and suggesting relationships between them, we are shaping that situation according to a way of thinking and to a purpose – i.e., we are in a process of evaluation. To relate this point to community development and the influence of community development workers, no such person comes neutral and value-free to any situation.

For instance, a social situation in a locality in the United States might be analyzed in terms of race and race discrimination. And the relationships between the people of different races might be stated in terms of change through conflict, or of the rightness of the *status quo*. Each of these sets of relationship between these elements implies a different purpose for the analysis: in the first case to arouse an awareness of common identity among certain people so that they may act together in a state of conflict (e.g., black power); in the second case, to persuade people to see a common and ordained interest in keeping things as they are and avoiding change (Ku Klux Klan). Such a model might then be generalized and used to analyze the situation in other places, such as Rhodesia or South Africa.

The use of such a model, and in fact the general usefulness of all models, can be approached in two ways. The first use can be called simple-minded, the second can be called creative.

By simple-minded I mean that someone simply takes an existing model as it stands, with its existing elements, relationships and values, and applies it unmodified to another situation, i.e., perceives situations uncritically in the image of the model. What has happened in this case is that the pattern of thinking and the purposes inherent in the model have simply been adopted without question. We can take an illustration of this approach from education. The predominant view of educational sociology is that between elements of society such as the political, economic, religious, and educational systems, the educational system is subordinate to the others – 'No educational institution can exert influences for change beyond those implied in its accepted function' (Brookover and Gottlieb, 1964,79). This view is illustrated in Figure 1.

And the majority of educationists in the administrative ranks of universities, government departments, teachers' federations, boards of education, accept this model and act according to it. They make their way by being proficient in the politics of the existing system. By so doing they fulfil and perpetuate the model. In this narrow sense, the usefulness of the model can be said to depend on the ability or inclination of its user to accept the elements and relationships set out in the model.

The second, or creative, way of using a model is to look at it within a different pattern of thinking, to re-examine and possibly reshuffle the elements and relationships. If, for instance, in the above example, educa-

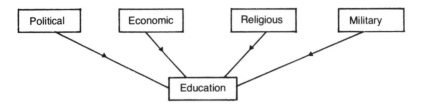

FIGURE 1   Relationships between education and other social spheres

tion is perceived not as subordinate to, but as counter to and subversive of the other systems, then other patterns of organization and other modes of action are prescribed for educationists. One does not then work to make the present education system more proficient at subordinating itself to other institutions. One works at alternatives to help people learn how to think and act critically (Vanek and Bayard 1975). In this sense the usefulness of the model lies in its suggesting a base from which alternative models can be formulated, in terms of different elements and/or different relationships.

One of the best examples of the critical and creative use of a model is the way Karl Marx took the dialectical model of philosophical thinking from Hegel and changed its elements to describe a historical process leading to the dictatorship of the proletariat. For Hegel the elements in the dialectical model, i.e., the thesis, antithesis, and synthesis, were abstractions; the process was a process of thought. For instance: theses = being, antithesis = nothing, synthesis = becoming; or thesis = inclination, antithesis = duty, synthesis = love. The dialectic was a process of reconciling opposites, which came to its culmination in an absolute and abstract idea. Marx, as has been said, took Hegel's dialectic and stood it on its head. For him material existence and modes of production determined spiritual, social, and political processes and the consciousness of people. The elements of the model for him become historical realities: thesis = capitalists, antithesis = workers, synthesis = the dictatorship of the proletariat. And the dialectic was not a reconciliation, but a repression of one by the other in all-out conflict, i.e., class warfare.

Chin distinguishes between analytical models and what he calls concrete models. Concrete models are based on analytical models, but they use the content of concrete cases (Chin 1964). For example, the small group process as a system can be seen as an analytical model, whereas the behaviour of a school committee as a small group can be seen as a con-

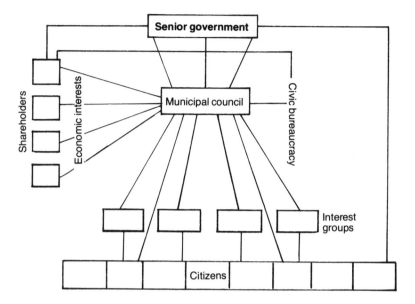

FIGURE 2 Elements in urban government: general

crete model. Homans makes a distinction which has similar elements, between analytical science and clinical science (Homans 1950,15). An analytical model in Homans' sense is general and abstract, i.e., the small group process, or the theory of blood chemistry, while a clinical model is related to a particular case, i.e., the behaviour of a school committee, or anaemia. Homans suggests that the important difference between analytical science and clinical science is that 'in action we must always be clinical. An analytical science is for understanding, but not for action, or at least not directly.' We may understand this to mean that when we intend to act we must come down to hard cases.

Figures 2 and 3 illustrate the difference between an analytical model and a concrete model. Figure 2 represents the typical elements in an urban centre, large or small, and the possible relationships between these elements in terms of power and influence.

In the middle is the elected governing body of the city – the council – which is the legally constituted body for making decisions which affect the lives of the people in that centre. On the other side are the individual citizens, who from time to time exercise their power to elect members of council , and in this respect they have a direct relationship with the council. In the long periods between civic elections, however, the citizens have practically no means of influencing decisions of council other than through a variety of intermediate groups formed around various interests or characteristics, such as cultural, religious, environmental, locality-based, ethnic, or income groups, including what in recent years have come to be called poverty groups. Any such groups commonly act in relation to council only when issues arise which affect them.

On another side are the business and industrial corporations with particular economic interests, such as land developers, speculators, downtown commercial businesses, and industrial companies. In one way or another these groups are in continuous contact with both the elected council and its supporting civic bureaucracy, with requests for rezoning, permits to build, requests for services, etc. and since much of the tax base of the city, and its general economic prosperity, depend on them, they have much influence. At the same time they are the employers of many of the citizens and have at all times a potential and sometimes an actual influence on these citizens. Behind them is the influence of their shareholders, some of whom are citizens of the city, while some are other companies and mutual funds who often have no local interest.

Above the city in the hierarchy of government is the provincial, state, or national government, which has influence and power through legislation, funding, and general economic development policies. The citizens have a periodic influence on these higher governments at election time, while the corporations, according to their importance in the national economy, have a more continuing influence.

These may be said to be the main elements in the scheme of things. To set them out in this way is to provide an *analytical* model by which to understand the forces that come into play in local government. But for groups of citizens who are confronted with a problem and who wish to influence decisions to overcome those problems, such a general analytical model has to be applied to the particular situation in the particular place. To take an example from the work of Alinsky, the model could be applied to the city of Rochester in New York State and adapted to symbolize the main elements and their relationships, as in Figure 3.

This *concrete* model illustrates the reality of Rochester as perceived by the Alinsky organization and the majority of the black citizens of the city. First, the citizens were clearly grouped into white and black, and the problems of poverty, unemployment, poor housing, etc., were preeminently problems of the black people. Secondly, Eastman Kodak dominated the life of the city, economically and culturally – through its support of the Univer-

City of Rochester

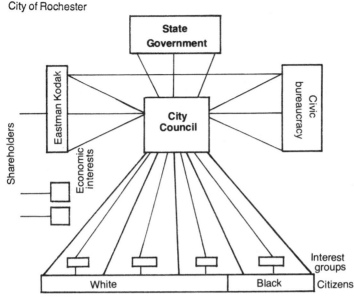

FIGURE 3   Elements in urban government: particular

sity, Museum, and symphony orchestra, of which the city was very proud. It was by identifying these two forces and concentrating on them among all the others that Alinsky formulated a strategy for change in that city. It was, for instance, in that city, from that particular situation, that Alinsky initiated the strategy of proxy voting in shareholders' meetings to confront the employment policies of Eastman Kodak. But Alinsky (1972,138) emphasized that particular situations must not be treated with prescriptions made up in other particular situations.

There is another interpretation of the term 'clinical model,' which acts as a bridge between analysis and action, and between the static and the dynamic. This interpretation sees the clinical model in terms of an on-going process, taking a situation as it is developing, observing it, diagnosing it, and taking a direct part in its development, as a psychotherapist takes a direct part in the process of a consultation with a client. Such a situation is open-ended in the sense that although the therapist, or community development worker, may have an idea in his own mind about where the case may lead, he is prepared to let it develop, to remain open-ended as long as possible, and to learn from it.

This sort of model changes the emphasis from an analysis of conditions at a point of time to an analysis of the process of change through a flow of time – a moving picture rather than a snapshot. It brings to the fore the idea of movement and change, of a dynamic condition rather than a static one and it is a condition to which a conceptual approach is not irrelevant. To quote Alinsky again, 'There are certain central concepts of action in human politics. To know them is basic to the pragmatic attack on the system. These rules make the difference between a realistic radical and a rhetorical one' (Alinsky 1970,xviii).

The emphasis shifts to an analysis of the elements and forces involved in change. Such structures are themselves conceptualizations, since it is *people* who change, and the relationships between people. Models which address themselves to process and flux are called process or developmental models.

Process models are based on the observation that society is a 'complex, multi-faceted, fluid inter-play of widely varying degrees and intensities of association and dissociation' (Buckley 1967,17). The emphasis shifts from the sets of relationships between elements in a structure to the way in which these relationships can change. If the relationship between two elements is altered, this alters all the relationships between all the elements. And so the emphasis moves from the static to the dynamic state. And more than that, the process model implies a different frame of mind, one in which the elements of a situation are perceived to move through various stages, levels, phases, and periods of change. It suggests ways of analyzing a flow of action. So the model of community development set out in diagrammatic form in Figure 4 in chapter 2 is a process model; it suggests a flow of behaviours on the part of persons involved in the process of community development, and it provides a series of bench marks by which people can provide feedback to themselves about such progress, or lack of it.

So just as it is suggested that we need both the analytical and the clinical approach in the range of our social acts, we also need analytical models. At one time we may want guidelines to help us to catch and understand the situation in a point of time: what elements exist in it, what values inform it, what institutions have what status in it, what is the human map? Analytical models may help us to order our perceptions into the form of a cognitive map. This is the approach in chapter 4. At another time we may want to make sense of what is going on within a group of people, what conflicts are being expressed, what leadership being shown, what emotional relationships are aiding or setting back the effectiveness of the group as a working unit. And this time process models may help us to order our observations into the form of a moving picture. This is the approach in chapter 5.

These questions lead to another: how do we choose the right model for the situation and thereby gain insight rather than fall into confusion and error? In arguing from the Kaplan analogy and discussing community development-in-use and reconstructions of community development, it was suggested that while the creation of the original act involves a kind of art, the adaptation of models of that act to new situations by other persons involves another kind of art on the part of these persons. Kaplan talks of the law of the instrument, that is, the tendency to use one model or technique with which one is familiar, or which one has used successfully in one situation, for all situations. In academic life where there are pressures to produce and become known by some distinctive theory or model, this danger is always present, and insofar as it is possible to lead an academic life without undue exposure to the practical effects of one's theories, it is a relatively harmless condition to continue in. But in the social and political affairs of human groups there is no such immunity; wrong judgments, and wrong actions in accordance with such judgments, can hurt people. Community development goes on in such a world, and people engaged in community development have to risk what in more academic circles tends to be disapproved of as the impurity of eclecticism.

CAUTIONS ABOUT THE USE OF MODELS

This discussion of the usefulness of models in community development leaves us with a few cautionary thoughts about the way models should be used. The first is that too great a reliance should not be placed on concrete models, i.e., specific cases in which particular institutions or groups of people behaved in a particular situation to produce particular outputs. Such models should be regarded with other models which analyze broader issues and suggest broader relationships of the elements involved.

Schon suggests not only a systems analysis approach, but the need for an existential approach to model building and social action. Since a changing situation contains more information than we can handle, we are, in effect, restricted to information in the here and now. While theories drawn from *other* institutions may provide perspectives or projective models for *this* situation which help to shape it and permit action within it, this process must grow out of the experience of the here-and-now and must be nourished and tested against it. In other words, we have to aspire to act as far as possible in the mode of the original artist, using our perceptions of current conditions.

The second caution about the use of models relates to Kaplan's reference to the law of the instrument. Actors in a process of social change, including community development workers, must extend their understanding to a repertoire of models, must come to be able to judge the appropriateness of particular models to particular situations, and must be flexible enough to move from one model to another as appropriate.

What is not required is the picking up by prospective community development workers of a bag of tricks for manipulating people without regard to the particular needs of different situations and, therefore, to the integrity and dignity of people with whom they work. The danger of this happening is not illusory when considered in the light of the training of community development workers and others in similar fields. There is evidence, for instance, in a field not exactly the same as community development but with some features of interpersonal relationships similar to those required in community development work, i.e., counselling and guidance, that university graduate education has the result of reducing some of the qualities important in interpersonal relationships in that field (Carkhuff and Berenson 1967,10-12). There is a tendency for the students to pick up 'professional' role behaviours that are not authentic because they fail to take into account differing realities. Moreover (and this relates back to the previous references to the role of the university) a study quoted by Carkhuff and Berenson (1967,10) indicates that the students who communicated the highest level of understanding of their clients' needs received the lowest grades in their training programs! Carkhuff and Berenson suggest that in training for counselling and guidance, theory and techniques can frustrate the whole object of the training. In the use of models in the work of community development, i.e., the way they are applied to the external situation, there is likewise a danger that the wrong use of the wrong models may frustrate the community development process. The models may also be used in a rigid, unimaginative way with the same results, or a poor understanding of these theories and models may mean a wrong use at a wrong time. Furthermore, a purely intellectual, or rote, knowledge of the models, may mean acting them out in such a way as to influence others adversely rather than favourably.

This leads to a third caution about the use of models, particularly when they are used in the designing of strategies for change. In chapter 2 it is suggested that one of the learnings which is necessary in the early stages of the community development process is that which relates to the self, and here we are concerned with the important element in community development work which has to do with the worker's self-understanding in the light of the demands which community development work is likely to make on him as a person. Experience indicates that an important part of the preparation of a community development worker should be learning about one's own values, personality, and motives. How much do I value other people's freedom to decide and act? How much am I seeking to control others? How much am I seeking human contact as a support, because of deep feelings of my own inadequacy? Why do I care? These are the sorts of questions that someone going into this field should ask himself, and learn the answers to, because the questions and the answers have a lot to do with effective interpersonal behaviour in groups, which is one necessary attribute of a community development worker.

Argyris and others working in the field of organization and administration stress the importance of self-understanding in bringing about effective interpersonal behaviour in organized groups. Argyris (1962,16-27) goes on to suggest that such behaviour is learned not so much by practice as by developing a correct Gestalt, which he defines as a cluster of values leading one to behave in specific ways. This still leaves a question as to how such values are themselves learned if they are not already there. What we are looking at here is the question of how individuals can come to see what values regarding human freedom and dignity are inherent in the ways they behave toward others, and what motives underlie such behaviour, and generally to understand themselves. In the model of the community development process proposed in chapter 2, I suggest that such learning on the part of the members of the emerging community is an important part of the total process, and what is now being suggested is that such learning is an important part in the preparation of the community development worker as well, from two points of view: first, to enable the worker to become a more effective person in his relationships with people in the community, and second, to be able to use, judiciously and appropriately, his knowledge of methods of self-understanding to help others to understand themselves better and become more effective actors in the community.

In practical terms, failure on the part of a community development worker to have really learned something about himself at both the cognitive and affective levels – how his behaviour affects other people and how to be honest in interpersonal relations – will negate whatever understanding he may have of models of the environment and of the appropri-

ateness of such knowledge to particular conditions. The community development worker has to work with and keep the confidence and trust of
people, and he can do this only if he acts authentically.

And it goes further. In discussing what he calls the expository model in
organization design, Vaill suggests that there are four kinds of data which
must be taken into account when a person or a group is designing strategies for change in a human system. The first is what he calls *science*, or
the findings that have been accumulated over years of research, knit together when possible in analytical models. The problem of designers of
new strategies is to use these findings in relation to data in other situations. The second is the present *situation*: the people involved, patterns of
relationships, the system's history, its operating characteristics, etc., and
this relates to Schon's suggestion about the need for an existential approach to model building and social action. Next are the *goals and norms*
of the system concerned. And finally – though Vaill does not put them in
this order – is the *self*: the personal abilities, values, and action-styles of
those involved in formulating new strategies. Vaill suggests that the expository model of science recognizes that questions about the self are
natural, but it proposes that they are at least irrelevant and perhaps
downright dangerous, for they indicate the presence of personal interest
and possibly of prejudice. And yet, Vaill suggests, they are fundamental
elements in the design of strategies in human affairs (Vaill 1974).

The final caution arises from observations which have been made of
the application of various strategies of social change in recent years. Some
of these have been concerned with the Model Cities, Office of Economic
Opportunity, and other such programs in the United States, and there has
been considerable analysis of the effectiveness of such programs. From
one such analysis, that made by Warren in 1974, it is possible to infer that
strategies of change and actions of change agents are often founded on
models based on values, assumptions, and perceptions of one social or
organizational group, and imposed upon other client groups. Models of
change proposed in these large American programs are generally the product of well-off, middle-class, power-holding groups, but are applied to
the problems of poor, powerless groups. They emphasize systems technology and forms of co-ordinated planning which do not appear to have
answered basic questions of power and poverty in contemporary American society (Warren 1974). On a wider front, models of economic development based on the experience of industrialized countries and the
assumptions of relatively free-enterprise capitalism, have been presumed
upon traditional rural economies in developing countries. This is an ap-

plication, at the international level, of the law of the instrument, but it raises the wider issue of the basic assumptions and values that are inherent in the formulation of models and consequent strategies of change. Here we are dealing with the issue of paradigms, i.e., patterns of thought within which approaches are made to social and political problems. The paradigm becomes not only the basis on which models are formulated but also the criterion for choosing problems that can be assumed to have solutions (Kuhn 1970,99). What Kuhn suggests of scientists, i.e., that they never learn concepts, laws and theories in the abstract, but within a historically prior unit of thought, appears to be valid for social change agents, and Kuhn goes on to suggest that like the choice between competing political institutions, that between competing paradigms proves to be a choice between incompatible modes of community life (ibid., 156).

This points to a need for a reasonably consistent use of some terms which I shall be using in this book: paradigms, models, and techniques. By 'paradigms' I shall mean a broad set of premises that shape our view of a significant part of the society in which we live; for example, that competition is natural and beneficial. I shall use the term 'model' in two ways, in relation to two levels of thought and action. Models of community development can be related to paradigms and can be classified according to broad characteristics, such as economic, cultural, educational, or political models. Within such broad models I will refer to narrower configurations of thought that help us order our courses of action, and these have been referred to as analytical and process models. The model of the community development process which I will propose in chapter 2 can be seen in these two senses. Within such models I shall refer to more specific 'techniques' that can be used, generally in conjunction with one another, to achieve specific objectives within the broader design of the model.

I have suggested that models have implied in them a certain way of thinking, certain purposes, and certain patterns of thought and systems of values. The central model in chapter 2 is no exception. It rests on the underlying propositions about the nature and capacity of people which are set out in the Preface. I indicate in various places in this book that it does not, however, rely on the acceptance of only one political and social system. With respect to the other models – and all models – what is important is the attitude and purpose with which they are approached. The attitude should be that they are not dogmatic but open-ended, and the purpose should be to enable people involved in the process of social action to be able to make good use of the resources available to them.

Using models is like using recipes. If the recipe calls for certain ingredients which one does not have, one tries something else in the kitchen. If one does not have the ingredients or the facilities, one does not use that recipe. But it happens; the danger is not illusory. It is illustrated by the case of an American home economist who came to Zambia to teach African women what was then called domestic science. In a new domestic science centre, with electrical gadgets such as stoves, mixers, refrigerators, etc., she tried to teach the recipe for Baked Alaska, which is a confection of angel cake and ice cream baked in a regulated oven. But her students came from rural villages where there was no electricity or running water and where people live a subsistence peasant life!

PART ONE

COMMUNITY, COMMUNITY DEVELOPMENT,
AND SOCIAL SYSTEMS

2

Community development: learning and action

THE CONCEPT OF COMMUNITY

THE CONCEPT OF COMMUNITY

As it emerged in a Conference on African Administration at Cambridge University, sponsored by the British Colonial Office in 1948, the term 'community development' had to do with emerging colonial states which were poor, predominantly rural, and lacking in sophisticated government machinery. Likewise, in the United States the term and the activity to which it is applied were closely related to the work of the International Co-operation Administration in predominantly rural overseas countries, while within the USA itself it was closely related to rural sociology. And this historical relationship appears to have carried with it a certain interpretation of the activity as a whole, and particularly of the term 'community,' as having to do with a fairly easily identifiable geographical locality.

This interpretation has persisted. As late as 1968, Sanders proposed that community development embodied two major ideas: (i) economic, technical, and social change (development), and (ii) locality, i.e., planned social change in a village, town, or city. And Rothman, describing three models of community organization practice, likewise equates community development with what he calls locality development (Rothman 1968).

In appendix A are set out a number of definitions which have been proposed at various times in various countries. In those definitions certain words have been underlined to point out what appear to be some common characteristics. One is that they tend to describe what the process of community development is, that is, what is supposed to happen, and they relate this process to such terms as 'community,' 'communities,' 'people,' and 'groups,' without defining these more closely. Only the Indian ones specify rural areas and organized village groups, and this indicates the focus of the activity in that country – though the use of the term 'village groups' appears to imply some set of groupings within the village, rather than the village as a whole.

The tendency to think in terms of geographical locality has two disadvantages. First, it is a tendency toward vagueness. Geographical locality may still provide the focus for initiative and action in relatively self-contained and small rural villages where isolation, or geographical features, define a problem, and even here, as one of the Indian definitions implies, it is likely that focused action requires a breaking down into smaller organized village groups. In large urban centres geography has little or no meaning except in cases where barriers such as freeways or railways isolate an area, but these are not so much problems of geography as of planning. Second, adherence to definition by geographical locality draws attention away from contemporary developments in communications which put people in close touch with one another even though they live some distance apart, from the broader context within which development takes place, and from the issue of power. Of all the definitions cited in appendix A, Bregha's is singular and significant in raising the question of the allocation of power as an important problem in community development.

In certain circumstances, in certain countries, where rural life revolves around villages that are relatively clearly demarcated, communities may be defined in a geographical way, but geography is not the important factor; the common interests, problems, and therefore objectives of the village people – objectives of better production methods, better marketing, better living standards, etc. – are what is important in identifying the community. Looked at from the point of a community development worker beginning work in such a village, or of a local leader concerned with the betterment of life in the village, the geographical factors will give no particular clues as to where to start unless they clearly create the problem. The clues lie in the perceptions of the problems facing the people and the groupings of people who are conscious of these problems. And an effective community begins to form only when objectives begin to be formulated around these problems. An indication in this direction appears in Hillery's analysis of ninety four definitions of community, where he found that the greatest area of agreement was around the possession of common ends, norms or means (Hillery 1955,111-23).

To whatever extent the definition of community may be related to geographical boundaries in such rural societies, this relationship is unrealistic in more complex urban life. Even where groups of people who live in urban ghettos come to articulate the kinds of needs which form the impetus for community development, a definition of that community by geographical factors would miss the point. The geographical identity of the group is secondary and largely consequent on other factors which form the basis of a common set of objectives in that group. There may not even be a common set of objectives; some of the people may have as their objective to leave the area as soon as possible and to join the general upward mobility enjoyed by other groups. And they will not identify with others in the ghetto who have as their objective the changing of the social system which imposes their existing conditions on them.

Objectives are not the same as issues. Alinsky points out that in a ghetto, different people have different issues which they want resolved: freedom from pimps and pushers, lower prices charged by local merchants, fair value appraisals for their hard won property (Alinsky 1972,76-8). These people become a community only when they can agree on common objectives in the form of a program of reform for their area.

An important element in this process of coming together around problems, is that of group identity. Among black and other minority groups in the United States, blacks in Rhodesia, native people in Canada, immigrant groups in Britain, a growing perception of their needs and problems merges into a perception of an identity shared by these people. Such a sense of identity is crucial in the movement toward a community and toward the formulation of objectives and a sense of power to do something about these objectives. For people who come to see themselves as deprived and powerless in the face of other people, one stage in the process of seeking change is to seek a base of support from which to move farther, and this base is seen to exist in a group of people in the same condition. At this stage of group identification it is common for there still to be no clear group objective; it is a matter of establishing a strong defensive position before feeling secure enough to plan and launch out further. This stage of establishing a group identity may be a long, groping, painful one, and it commonly draws criticism from other people and other groups expressed in such terms as, 'but you don't even know what you represent?' It is only when there is some sense of identity and the objectives have a mutual relationship that a community begins to form. While objectives are in the course of being formulated, something social is happening, but until the objectives are formulated, and accepted, it is doubtful that there is a community. So the community exists when a group of people perceives common needs and problems, acquires a sense of identity, and has a common set of objectives. Thus a profession may be a community despite its lack of a 'physical locus' (Rubin 1969).

Most of the groups referred to above are large. They are not identifiable in geographical terms except in a most general way, that is, that they live in a certain part of the world. If local geographical boundaries were to be a necessary element in the definition of a community, these could not be called communities. But one element in the consideration of a unit called a community is communication – the ability of people to communicate with one another. Without this it is not practicable to formulate and agree on objectives. So, again, in developing countries with poor transport and communication facilities, it is reasonable that communities tend to be small primary groups and their immediate neighbours. But in modern industrialized societies, communication is not necessarily a face-to-face business. Nor is it in many other countries where radio, television, and telephone, quite apart from the press and the postal service, are a normal part of life. As Marshall McLuhan and Barbara Ward suggest, the earth itself is a global village. More and more information becomes available to more and more people; the problem is how to use it properly. Common objectives can be formulated between people not in continuous personal contact, and if means of transportation make it possible for these people – or enough of them to matter – to meet periodically face to face to consolidate affairs, then agreements and decisions can be reached. The extent to which this can happen and a community can, in fact, be formed, will depend on the extent to which the group can establish internal qualities which are referred to later in the discussion of the process of development.

The white authorities in South Africa and Rhodesia know very well the importance of communication, both in the formation and maintenance of communities, and in the linking of communities into wider coalitions. They know that one way to stop any real development is to take control as far as possible of the channels of communication, and so in South Africa radio and television are controlled by the government. In Rhodesia, both radio and television are tightly controlled by the white regime through the Rhodesian Broadcasting Corporation. In both countries the mails and telephone service are subject to interception when any 'subversive' communication is suspected. And to minimize the opportunities of action there is a tight control of the movement of people through pass laws, police checks and swift and arbitrary detention. I was involved in an experience while working in Rhodesia, when the night before a group of black trade union leaders were due to travel to the capital, Salisbury, for a weekend workshop on organization, they were rounded up by the police and detained without charge for the weekend, and then released at the end of it. This happened on two consecutive weekends, thus frustrating this attempt to get some of the black leaders together. Other black leaders have not been as lucky and have been held in detention without trial for years.

Despite measures of this sort, it is not easy to prevent all communication in circumstances like this. In late 1971 and early 1972, white Rhodesians were surprised and chagrined to see the emergence of a coherent black opposition in the country to proposals for a constitutional settlement reached between the white regime and the British government. Much of this opposition had been arranged at the local community level, and here was an example of strong local interests and objectives coalescing in a wider course of action.

In other words, communication is effected not just through formal, controllable channels. Underground channels – grapevines – are formed; it is impracticable to stop all movement of people, even as it was in Nazi-occupied Europe. And this will be the more likely to happen where the majority of people share the same interest. In the Rhodesian situation it is because of the almost complete lack of communication between whites and blacks (relationships are, with a miniscule exception, on a master-servant basis) that the whites could be so deluded about black feelings and intentions.

We are facing, therefore, the possibility, in certain circumstances, of an extension of the concept of community development from that of relatively tightly connected local groupings to that of groups dispersed over wide areas. The establishment and the work of the Northwest Territories Indian Brotherhood which is spread over a vast area of northern Canada, can be considered as an exercise in community development, and the Brotherhood can be considered a community. This is happening mainly because of easier communication, but also because experience begins to show that many issues such as native rights, poverty, unemployment, poor housing, and alienation are so wide as not to be amenable to resolution at a local level. It has even been suggested, for instance, that community development in Britain is not likely to achieve much unless it is recognized that the real problems facing those people living in certain circumstances to which community development has traditionally been attracted, are not local, or 'community' ones, but 'class' ones – and working class at that (Jackson 1973). One interpretation of the Rhodesian problem, based on a Marxist analysis, suggests the same for that country (Arrighi 1966). Whether one adopts such a Marxist approach or not, certainly in the post-industrial world social units sharing a common and

particular interest, and capable of being in close communication and formulating clear objectives, are likely to be larger than those in less 'advanced' countries (Etzioni 1968,11). A distinction must still be made,
however, between these particular groupings and the whole state em-
bracing them. There is still a distinction between community development and the management of national and provincial affairs in general.

Nor does this say that smaller, closer groupings in small areas no longer
exist or are no longer relevant to the discussion of community development. Groups such as tenants associations in Britain and voluntary groups
with some sort of social orientation in Canada and the USA, and communes do exist, and formulate social objectives and work toward them.
Because they are not tackling the big problems – problems that have roots
going deeper and wider in society – they are not to be excluded as instruments of community development. Their success will be assessed by
them in terms of their objectives, and if the achievement of these objectives reveals further tensions and the need to have further objectives,
then the process may continue. What is being suggested is that both those
who are studying community development and those who are engaged in
it, should first, not locate communities by geography, but by interest and
objectives and, second, be aware that in times of constant information
flow, the notion of community may be greatly extended. What can begin
to emerge in the United States, for example, is the formation of coalitions
of community groups, such as the Community Congress in San Diego,
which links Black, Chicano, Filipino, and Asian groups and has set up,
among other things, a joint project for training community workers for all
the participating groups.[1]

There is one further point about the concept of community. Objectives
change, or rather, within a set of superordinate goals – what Alinsky calls
the top value – objectives keep being superseded by new ones, either in
the course of their being pursued or upon their failing to be achieved or
upon their achievement. It is a common experience of those involved in
voluntary associations formed with particular aims and not just to answer
the needs of companionship, that after a period of active life during which
problems are discussed, plans made, an organizational form worked out,
and many of the aims achieved, the life of the association begins to flag;
the membership falls off, office-holding becomes a bore, or a sinecure, or
both, or internecine disputes break out. It is often into such a situation

1   I am indebted to my friend, Anne Dosher, for this information. See also *Journal of
    Alternative Human Services* 2, no. 1 (April-June 1976)

that a community worker is invited by some of the members of the association who want help in reviving it. And it could well be that in most such cases, the right course would be to let the old association die and to form a new one with people who have needs as a base for new objectives. There are many moribund community organizations.

In the same way, a community as we have defined it may become moribund. And this need not be a matter for mourning. Bennis and Slater note that we are increasingly faced with the need to learn how to operate and live in temporary systems or societies, and to cope with the psychological problems of moving from one society to another. And this has some bearing on the kind of relationship that should exist between individuals and the communities with which they identify themselves (Bennis and Slater 1969,77-96). Individuals belong to a number of groups at the same time, each meeting a different need; likewise it is reasonable that needs shared by groups of individuals should be met by their forming successions of communities each with feasible objectives.

This concept of community differs from the widely accepted one which is exemplified by, and may stem from, the concept suggested by McIver in the 1920s. According to this concept, community has a permanence; it is a focus for social life, the 'common living of social being.' McIver made the distinction between such an entity and an association, which was an organization established for the pursuit of one or more common interests. While the association was partial, the community was integral (McIver 1924,22-4). Under this interpretation the community remains a looser, more tenuous linkage of people and organizations, an implicit social phenomenon rather than an explicit entity on the lines suggested above. The argument for this is that such a concept of community avoids bringing everything into a structured and relatively formal relationship; it maintains an ideal of freedom for people, outside the various formal institutions but still within a kind of framework that gives some sense of security and social belonging. It also allows one to propose a framework, a system, within which the holistic approach to social and environmental problems may be made, as distinct from fragmented approaches which may result from activities of the object-forming and object-seeking type of community discussed in this chapter. Those who hold to this interpretation of the term 'community' would consider the kind of grouping suggested above to be more the nature of an association or agency rather than a community.

McIver's concept of a wider implicit social phenomenon accords with the views of many writers who distinguish between action at a community level and action of a more restricted nature. For instance, Verner (1971) distinguishes between action at the small group level, the sub-organizational level, and the organization level, and action at these levels he calls social action, as distinguished from community action which is action involving the whole community. He does not, however, define community. There are too many places in too many parts of the world that do not offer that framework of security and social belonging which is the important element in the McIver concept, and where there is, there-fore, no reality which corresponds to that concept. Slater suggests that contemporary American society, for example, actively frustrates any feel-ing or desire which people may have for such a sense of community (Slater 1970). Young and Willmott have discovered the lack of such community among former east Londoners removed to new centres in England (Young and Willmott 1957). Without such a reality it is difficult to see what com-munity development can be related to, what clarity there can be for the initiation and purpose of the process of community development. It is likely that it is because of an attachment to such an affectively attractive concept, but illusive state of being, that a great deal of community development effort, particularly in rapidly changing and disintegrated centres of popula-tion, has not succeeded.

Two comments should be made on this line of argument. The first is that insofar as the McIver concept of community implies a warning against fragmented efforts to change and improve the condition of certain groups without regard to a general improvement in the environment, it has great relevance. A process of objective-forming and action which is turned inward to one group or community in the sense we have sug-gested, and excludes consideration of other communities, and the envi-ronment, is unlikely to serve the interests of that group or of others in the environment and is likely to fail in its objectives, for it would leave out of account the forces in the environment which affect the process. The ne-cessity to take into account the systemic relationship of communities and their environments is examined in more detail in chapter 3 where models based on systems theory, and the relationship of communities to social systems, are discussed.

The second comment is connected to this first one, in that it has to do with the relatedness of people and groups in the larger social context. The argument put forward in the preceding pages is not meant to suggest the perpetuation of the sort of dichotomy which is described in the two terms, 'the missing community' and 'the great society.' In discussing these two terms in relation to the education system, Newman and Oliver go back to the Tönnies idea of Gemeinschaft. A community is an organic, natural set of relationships, a group in which membership is valued as an end in itself; which concerns itself with many significant aspects of the lives of members; which allows competing factions; whose members share commitment to a common purpose and to procedures for handling conflict in the group; whose members share responsibility for actions of the group; and whose members have an enduring and extensive personal contact with each other (Newman and Oliver, 1967). They contrast this with mass society, which is mechanical and rational, and which is characterized by fragmentation of life, by change, ideological and aesthetic bankruptcy, depersonalization and powerlessness. And they suggest reforms in education, designed to revitalize community life by restoring a natural flow of learning which uses *all* the human and institutional resources of the community, not just the schools – a concept which now goes under the name of community education. Having defined community along Tönnies' lines, they are left, however, with the admission that it will be difficult in practice to restore the missing community to contemporary life. They propose in a normative sense what community *should* be, as a means of restoring qualities of human relatedness, but when they come to give examples of ways in which this may be done, the examples come down to the identification of groups which have common interests and objectives: ghetto parents wanting better education for their children; radio hams interested in electronics; industrial workers with common concerns about their plant; southern workers wanting to unionize. In other words, Newman and Oliver come in the end to a position much the same as that set out in our discussion of the concept of community.

That discussion and that concept does not rule out a search for the sort of community wanted by Newman and Oliver, and by many others. For it leads to a consideration of the relationship of communities and social systems, in chapter 3.

THE MEANING OF DEVELOPMENT

The definitions cited in appendix A reveal another characteristic of community development, which is an emphasis on the initiative and participation of people in defining their 'felt needs' and in doing something about meeting them by being involved in a problem-solving process (though one of the Canadian and British definitions admits that if this initiative 'is not forthcoming spontaneously, then techniques for arousing and stimulating it must be utilized'). It is this characteristic which appears, at any rate in the past, to have been used to distinguish community development from other processes that go under such labels as 'community organization' and 'social work' where the initiative is seen as coming more often than not from some agency apart from the people whose needs are at issue. In recent years the distinction between these terms, and what they represent, appears to have blurred.

THE PROCESS OF DEVELOPMENT

What is worth pursuing as part of a discussion of the term 'development' is the relationship between community development and adult education. Development in the present context does not mean maturation – the natural process of individual growth, so we are not concerned here with the human group in which such growth primarily takes place, the family and kinship group. Nor does it have the meaning given it in theories of social evolution, i.e., social change as gradual, continuous and an inherent characteristic of society moving toward the degree of perfection which for many writers in the nineteenth century and later was represented by Western industrial society (Nisbett 1969,189). As Nisbett suggests, we cannot assume that historical, finite, identifiable communities have those indigenous properties that lead to an ideal social condition which was always latent in them. An important feature of community development is its assumption that man must take a hand, that he is a necessary and capable partner in the shaping of his life and the life of the society he lives in. In other words, it assumes a capacity for and a process of learning.

It has been suggested earlier that the process of development starts with the perception of a problem or need on the part of people. In fact, the process can be said to begin before that with the feeling of unease or tension about one's condition, without a clear awareness of what causes the feeling. The next step in the process is to identify what is causing the feeling, i.e., what is the problem. To use Maslow's terms, this may reflect a deficient need or a growth need (Maslow 1968,chap. 3). The process starts either with the existence of deficiencies in social conditions, such as poverty, unemployment, or bad housing, or with some more positive goals. On the one hand, for instance, poverty arises out of a clear deficiency in the resources of people to keep themselves physically and mentally healthy and economically secure. The problem in such a condition will be to get to the root of such deficiencies and to overcome them. On the other hand people have a capacity for striving for certain goals without the impetus of deficiencies: a group of citizens whose basic economic and social needs are being met may feel a need for greater enrichment in their cultural life. In both these kinds of situation, a tension arises, and this tension becomes a creative force.

The process then involves learning on the part of the people in the group and, if possible, on the part of other groups which may be involved: learning about the individuals themselves – by the individuals themselves – about the group and about their environment. This in itself entails learning skills of communication by members of the group. When, as a result, there is a clearer understanding of their attitudes toward one another and toward others outside the group, the question arises 'Where do we go from here?' By going through a process of group discussion, a set of objectives is formulated. At this stage it can be said that the group becomes a community; it shares not merely an awareness of tensions, but a conscious set of objectives which clarify the very identity and membership of the group. But while a community does not become a reality until a group of people have succeeded in agreeing on objectives, a process of development is taking place before the community is thus established. Development includes the prior process in which the initial problems and tensions are worked through by the people concerned and an identity of objectives is established and a community is formed. Community development therefore includes in its early phase a process of community creation.

To realize these objectives, further learning is necessary: skills such as organization and administration (including possibly such apparently simple skills as record keeping). These skills place the community in a position of being able to take action to achieve its objectives.

Then follows evaluation, which is the process by which the community assesses the extent to which it has achieved its objectives. And this can bring out further tensions which can start off another cycle of development. The consequence of social change can be tension-producing as well as tension-reducing (Moore 1963,11).

This model of the community development process is set out in graphic form in Figure 4.

The relationship between adult education and community development may be found along the continuum which extends from learning about oneself, one's group and one's environment, to action and evaluation. Adult education could be thought of as having to do with the individual, since learning is an individual process, while community development might be thought of as having to do with the group or community. Thus the distinction might be made – as Katz and Kahn (1966,391-2) make it – between in-

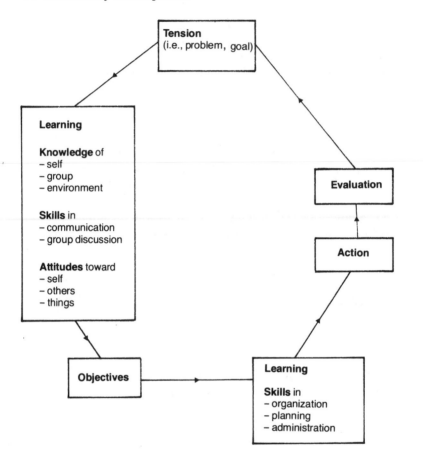

FIGURE 4 Model of the community development process

dividual change and 'the modification of organizational variables.' But Katz and Kahn go on to point to the psychological fallacy of concentrating on individuals without regard to the role relationships that constitute the social system of which they are a part. They also point to the complementary sociology fallacy of assuming that *any* alteration in human behaviour can be brought about in organizations provided that the process of change is initiated with due attention to organizational structure. In other words, the relationship between individual behaviour and social structure is a complex one.

Whereas a conceptual distinction might be made between self-knowledge, self-control, and self-development on one hand, and knowledge, control, and development of one's environment on the other hand, this cannot be made the basis for a distinction between adult education and community development. To equate community development with the knowledge, control, and development of one's environment, without taking into account the need for self-knowledge, self-control, and self-development, is to deprive community development of an important element. The development of the community involves the development of the individuals, of their personal insights, and of their understanding of who they are.

This view is borne out by experience. Among groups of people who become aware of a lack of participation in the decision-making processes of their society, and who get together in one way or another to try to rectify this, what starts off as a concern to influence the social and political circumstances 'out there,' sooner or later takes on the other dimension of a concern to get to know and develop oneself, to know the limits and potential of one's own capacities. This is a reason why in community development there is a good deal of interest in group processes, interpersonal relationships, and personal growth, and the kinds of training and experience with which one is able to learn about these subjects. This interest and these processes are often a part of the larger process of establishing group identity which has been referred to above.

Adult education may be said to be concerned with the process and the outcomes of learning – *process* in the sense of how people learn, and how to bring about the experiences and the environment in which they learn; and *outcomes* in the sense of the knowledge, skills, and attitudes which are acquired in the process. Ideally understood and practised, education is concerned not simply to take *a priori* assumptions or inclinations and to establish a rationale for them, and skills to implement them, but to start with states of tension and to examine them, look all around them, see them and test them in relation to others, and investigate alternative ways of bringing them to a resolution. It is certainly an activity in which the educator, or animator has no right to impose his own assumptions on the people with whom he works; he should be there to help them to understand their own potential and examine alternative ways of resolving them. From then on, they may make their own choices, and this includes choices of action. And it is at this stage that the emphasis changes from that of education to community development. In other words, community development adds an outcome of action to a process of learning. Adult education is a part of that process: learning, action, reflection, evaluation, revision of action, and so on. The relationship of education to community development has to do with the relationship of learning to social change.

Regarding the work in this process of agents from outside the group, there is a place for two roles: that of educator and that of activist, and the performance of the two roles by one person raises for that person a question of integrity which he has to cope with. To talk about remaining as far as possible in the role of educator and not becoming engaged in action, is not the same as saying that the agent must remain entirely neutral or objective, even if this were humanly possible. It does, however, seem possible and useful for there to be available to the group a resource person committed not to action on his part, but to learning toward action on the part of the group, that is, to their acquiring knowledge of themselves as a group, of their environment, and of alternative choices of decision. The element of learning which has to do with skills in the context of social change brings the two roles of educator and activist together. For the skills in question include those of communication, organization and administration, which are part of the action. The French term 'animation sociale' seems appropriate here.

Reverting for a moment to the model of the community development process: the arrest of that process at this stage of learning is an arrest of the process of community development. For instance, people may come to feel tensions arising out of some social problem, and they may begin to look around for knowledge of a sort that will help them to resolve these tensions. They may join education programs in such subjects as economics, politics, history, sociology, etc. or they may join group discussions, or attend sensitivity training laboratories, with a range of purposes from personal growth to the study of group processes. If they become settled in such learning experiences, then there will be no process of community development. Worthwhile personal development may well take place, but it is also possible that something like an escape into mysticism may take place.

If, on the other hand, there is a leap-frogging from the stage of tension to the stage of action, without a process of learning and the formulation of clear objectives, what then happens is not community development but precipitate action which, without the intervening and sometimes long process of investigation and learning, commonly leads to unsatisfying outcomes. Africa in the late 1950s and 1960s showed many half-done and abandoned projects in the form of clinics, community halls, ground nut schemes, started before the people were convinced they needed them. In

Canada we have projects like co-operative saw-mill operations in areas of native settlement which have failed for lack of preparatory study, and dams, such as the Bennett Dam in northern British Columbia, which have caused serious unanticipated problems for lack of adequate consideration of ecological matters. These are examples of the economic model of development, a characteristic of which is a preconception of the solution before the problem has been properly identified – a characteristic of the paradigm of western industrial society. The educational model of development sees the solution (which may in the end be economic) as emerging from the process of learning outlined in the model proposed above.

Precipitate action is often a sign of what Mannheim refers to as Utopianism, in which certain oppressed groups are intellectually so strongly interested in the destruction and transformation of a given condition or society, that they become incapable of correctly diagnosing it; 'their thought is never a diagnosis of the situation, it can be used only as a direction for action' (Mannheim 1936,40). And Alinsky (1972,185), no slouch at action, says, 'he [the community worker] must *know* if he is to organize.' He must know the values and problems, the way of life in the environment which he seeks to change. Moreover, the concept of community development has in it an important assumption which is that the action is not violent but can be carried through by a social process. This implies a society which will tolerate local groups which set out to formulate objectives involving changes in their conditions of living. Alinsky suggests with regard to India that Gandhi's ability to use non-violence depended upon the relative tolerance of his efforts by the British government. In a society which is not of this sort, a society in which government is in the hands of persons or groups who will not allow effective local decision-making and action, community development in these terms is not really possible. Thus, in Rhodesia, though community development has been professed as a part of government policy since the late 1950s and in spite of the definition as set out in appendix A, what goes by the name of community development is a kind of administrative device which ostensibly involves groups of rural Africans in the government process, but in fact denies them such a part and keeps real control with white officials working under a government elected by a white minority (Government of Rhodesia 1965).

It would certainly be stretching too far the concept of community development to apply it to movements, clandestine or not, which go through a process of learning and decision-making to violent confrontation or evolution. But to be talking about community development is not to be holding it out as the only valid kind of social and political change.

It becomes a nicer matter to decide how far community development is really possible in a society which holds itself to be democratic, but where control, both local and central, is exercised by representatives of a majority group. This condition is seen to exist in Britain by Hill and Issacharoff (1971,260), in the United States by Marris and Rein (1969,164-90) and in Canada by many native people.

The implication in this line of thought is that the community development *process* is predominantly a political one, even though there may be cultural and spiritual elements to it, and even though the goals may in some instance be cultural and/or spiritual.[2]

For Deutsch the increase in power to change the environment is one of four dimensions of growth in a community, or elements in its development. The other three are: an increase in *openness*, i.e., in the channels by which the group receives input from the outside world: an increase in inner *complementarity* or coherence, i.e., in the transfer of information from one part of the group to others; and an increase in *learning capacity*, including a capacity to change its own objectives. (Deutsch 1952). The three latter qualities affect the relationships between the members of the groups; they are internal to the group, and the models in subsequent chapters are addressed mainly to this aspect of the community development process. But these internal qualities are important for the group's power to act on its environment.

GOALS AND PARADIGMS OF DEVELOPMENT

A feature of community development is that it assumes a capacity in people to conceive general goals as well as intermediate objectives. In other words, while in the immediate and narrow sense it can be said that achieving the successive objectives set by the community in question is

2 As a way of initiating a discussion on the meaning of community development and of students' perceptions of and attitude toward it, and of forming a quick group profile of such perceptions and attitudes, I have occasionally listed pairs of adjectives such as 'hard/soft,' 'authoritarian/permissive,' 'autocratic/democratic,' 'oral/anal,' 'cognitive/ affective,' 'warm/cold,' 'hot/cool' (à la McLuhan), 'liberal/conservative,' Consciousness II/Consciousness III (à la Reich), 'scientific/humanistic,' 'classical/romantic' (all of which become very loaded terms in our common use of them), and have asked students to choose the one word from each of the pairs which comes closest to describing their feeling about community development and the nature of the work in the field. The discussion of the resulting profiles, and of the tone of the whole group's perception which comes out of them, more or less clearly, can be a useful base from which to proceed into a study of the subject.

what community development is about, a characteristic of the philosophy of community development is that it looks beyond these intermediate objectives to a broader condition of life. It is not a hasty choosing of objectives which, although they may be attractive in a short run or in a material sense, are likely to be ultimately destructive. It is a process of learning about people and their environment, and making decisions aimed at their continuing development. This implies a view of the nature and capacity of man: that he is not only goal-seeking, but order-seeking; that not only can he set objectives in company with others, but that he can see these objectives in relation to a wider order of things, a broader social plan. Development is, therefore, a process of making rational social choices and of improving the ability of groups of people to make such choices, to implement them, to judge their outcomes, and to revise them so that the condition of life improves.

When we come to discuss goals, we are concerned with two conditions: the condition of life within the community itself and the condition of the environment in which the community exists. From the point of view of those who see the solution in a communitarian life style, the quality of the internal communal life of the group is paramount, and the goal is harmony, charity, and a reasonable standard of living *within* the group. Most of them would probably deny the political attribution to the community development process which has been made above, but there seems clear evidence that it is the lack of such political dynamics – collective goal-setting and goal-attainment, and effective organization and decision-making – that has caused so many communes to fail. They have failed to realize that whatever non-political, spiritual ends they have in mind, the attainment of those ends is a political process. As Musgrove suggests in his study of the counter-culture and some communes in Britain, 'even sharing needs some organization. There is a tendency for the milk bottles never to be put out' (Musgrove 1974,198).

With regard to Deutsch's four dimensions of growth, most supporters of communal living would very likely deny the need for, or the aspiration toward, an increase in power to change the environment. But there are some who do see such a life style as an influence for, and source of, change in society in general. It is clear, for instance, that communities such as Findhorn in Scotland, Lindisfarne in New York, Auroville in India, see themselves as having an influence on people and life styles in the world outside. Findhorn, for instance, in acquiring a nearby hotel to accommodate guests, sees it as a 'challenge for us to deepen our commitment to pioneering a vision of education and demonstration in the New Age' (Findhorn 1976).

More generally, Musgrove sees the counter-culture, including its communal groups, as being in a dialectical relationship with main-stream society, each transforming the other (Musgrove 1971,16-18).

Insofar as a goal is an end state or condition to which one aspires, the goals of development are frequently expressed in terms which have political connotations, e.g., freedom for all individuals and societies, and freedom from servitude considered to be oppressive (Goulet 1971). Even if they are expressed in economic terms, e.g., a better standard of living for people, or cultural terms, e.g., stronger ethnic identity through traditional ethnic arts, the attainment of such goals affects other communities and thus has political repercussions, which in turn lead to political limitations on the possibility of their attainment. Development in this sense is a challenge to the established order; it is thus that Goulet, speaking about development in a world context, suggests that 'development ethics must contest the established order, which is the order of under-development for the majority of men in the world' (Goulet 1971,119). It is in the same context that Dom Helder Camaro, the Brazilian church leader, prefers to speak of liberation rather than development (Camaro 1975).

Such an analysis suggests, within the present framework of things, severe limitations of community development as a process of changing the broad economic and political environment. It is, in fact, marginal to the main process of social and political change – the possible exception to this being the impact of the sort of community-by-long-range-communication, e.g., the Northwest Territories Indian Brotherhood, which has been referred to earlier. And even here the ultimate influence for change will depend upon the power which such a community can come to command, or can be perceived as commanding, and/or on the attitude or frame of mind of the controlling elements in society. If such communities can attract enough support, they may be instrumental in effecting substantial political and social changes, and it is possible to argue that nationalist parties in black Africa in the 1960s were initially communities that went through a development process and achieved more than marginal change. But it is also possible to argue that they were able to do so because of a shift in the pattern of thinking of the metropolitan countries, i.e., in a growing acceptance on the part of these countries in a changing world climate toward colonialism, of the inevitability and the practicability of independence for their colonies.

Indeed, it is not outrageous to suggest that until this acceptance became an element in the policy of the metropolitan countries, community development was a government-supported strategy for keeping the natives happy without substantial changes. Nor is it outrageous to suppose that the Northwest Territories Indian Brotherhood's goals of self-determination for northern native people and economic control over the land they live on, are not likely to be achieved within the present value system which lays stress on resource development for the benefit of industry in other parts of North America, and on the interests of white-dominated corporate enterprise. The situation basically is not far removed from that in Rhodesia where community development has had to operate within the paradigm of white-dominated society and is not allowed to disturb it.

Which is to suggest that the marginality of community development and its relative ineffectiveness as a process of wide change or as an influential element in the whole political system is related to the dominant political and social paradigm in which it operates. It is right for Newman and Oliver (1967), in their discussion of education and community, to suggest the need for a revival of the missing community (and not just as an exercise in nostalgia), to counteract the mass society of industrialization, urbanization, technology, etc. But it is precisely in such a mass society with its values based on economic returns, largeness of scale, multinational corporations and international decision-making, and the remote rule of 'experts' that tolerance for and effectiveness of community endeavor is unlikely. And this is Goulet's point about development being a challenge to the established order.

What writers such as Reich (1970), Roszack (1969), Curle (1972), Musgrove (1974), and Trist (1968) are suggesting is that perhaps there are signs of change in the paradigm, or signs of a new paradigm appearing in the affluent countries of the west. Their perceptions are of a condition in which sharing and co-operation will be counter-values to exploitation and competition, in which organic forms and collaborative relations will be the dominant organizational philosophies, rather than mechanistic forms and competitive relations, and in which interdependence will predominate as a cultural value over independence and achievement. These are the features of the post-industrial society, and they are features which on the face of it look more congenial to the sort of philosophy and practice that is represented by community development. In the east the Chinese version of communism can be interpreted as another alternative society in which collectivism is organic, incorporating much of the traditional groupness of Chinese life, in which men are social beings and citizens first and individuals second, and in which an undoubted pursuit of technology appears yet to be tempered by traditional values of collaboration, interdependence, and organic harmonies.

This puts us at the junction between the optimism which is engendered by such perceptions and the starker perception of Ellul (he rejects the possible charge of pessimism) in which technological society – the mass society – is not to be redeemed. And it is likely that a choice between the two ways is to be made not by the intellect alone but by a compound of intellect, phenomenological 'facts,' and value judgments – or just plain faith. ¶Though Ellul (1964,xxviii) suggests that his judgments are based upon previous metaphysical value judgments, one may question such a confident distinction. In any case, Ellul accepts that the continued excesses of technology might be forestalled by the emergence of new phenomena outside the range of his sociological analysis. And one of these is the increasing awareness by more people of the threat which the technological world poses to man's personal and spiritual life, and their determination to assert their freedom by upsetting the course of this evolution (ibid., 1964,xxx). And such a rejection of the existing societal paradigm can itself be one important quality that identifies and defines a community.

So we are left in the end to make our own interpretation and judgment. Observation of contemporary mid-1970s political and economic affairs shows few of the qualities of that predicted post-industrial society. Nevertheless, community development is not to be entirely scorned as a mode of political behaviour, for it is based on a concept which stresses the importance of the presence, between the individual on the one hand and the continuing units of the state on the other, of intervening structures which engage people in learning and formulating social and political objectives, and in this way 'drag them into the torrent of social life' (Rubin 1969,113). Brokensha (1974) points out that despite the failure of community action in the Office of Educational Opportunity and Model Cities Program in the usa, there were some dividends: these programs did unleash forces of social action; they helped the poor to gain self-confidence and self-respect, to learn about organizing and to establish pressure groups; and this caused agencies to be more aware and sensitive to the needs of people in poor communities.

Though the community development process will continue to be political, there are signs that more people are seeing the ends as more than economic and material. And though the ability to exercise power will continue to be an important element in the process, there are signs that people are gaining power from sources other than economic dominance.

3

Communities and social systems

If, as in chapter 2, a community is defined in such a way as to allow it to be identified with what McIver (1924) calls an association, i.e., a partial and tenuous linkage of people for a particular purpose, this might be thought to be fragmenting social life intolerably. But it was suggested that there was a linkage between such communities and their environment, and it is these linkages that I want to clarify before going on to suggest some models which relate to the community development process.

My definition turns the community from being an implicit, integral, permanent focus of social life, 'the common living of social being,' generally with some degree of geographical identity, into something which can in one sense be greater than this and in another sense less than it. I have suggested that for the purposes of community development, a community has to be seen as a collection of people who have become aware of some problem or some broad goal, who have gone through a process of learning about themselves and about their environment, and have formulated a group objective.

This can be greater than the community in the more traditional view, in the sense that these days such a group of people can be spread over many distant places and still be closely in touch and be able to plan and to act in concert. One example given earlier is the Northwest Territories Indian Brotherhood. Others might be an international aid agency such as OXFAM, or a professional group such as the Canadian Medical Association.

A community in terms of this definition can be less than the traditionally defined community in the sense that it can consist of a relatively small group of people forming an organization, or system, within what is traditionally seen as the community – for instance, a housing co-operative, or a tenants' association.

This difficulty of definition seems to beset the use of the concept, 'community,' in Warren's treatment of the subject, particularly as it relates to community development (Warren 1963). Warren devotes much of his book to attempting to reconcile the concept of social systems and the traditional concept of community proposed by writers such as McIver. While Warren holds that geographic interrelationships are still important, the psychological boundaries still exist in some communities, and that there is often a sense of identification with one's community (1963,15), he admits that as a great change transforms American communities, increasing impersonality and bureaucracy, among other variables, operate to place increasing importance on the organization to which individuals belong (1963,chap. 3). And finally, he admits that 'the next decades may see far-reaching reorganization in community theory caused not only by the rapid changes which are transforming the nature of communities, but also by the mature re-examination of some of the relatively naive conceptions of the community as a social phenomenon which have characterized much previous investigation' (1963,339).

What Warren calls naive conceptions of the community might, alternatively, be called romantic in the sense of being somewhat remote from the experience of a great part of humanity which lives in a lonely crowd, and nostalgic in the sense of reflecting back on a folk life which for such people no longer exists. I am proposing that the re-examination of which Warren speaks must include consideration of community development in more hard-headed terms of effective social and political behaviour, that is, the effective behaviour of groups of people in pursuit of a better condition of life.

Warren brings us to a consideration of the relationship between communities and social systems. For systems theory and analysis directs attention both to the internal functions and relationships which identify an organization or community, i.e., a system, and to the relationships between the system and its environment. Its application to community development helps us to understand the internal nature and dynamics of a community, as well as its connections with the society in which it exists.

Internally, systems thinking helps us to see the community not merely as an aggregate or a summation, in which the parts, i.e., the members, are added to one another and continue to function because of their inherent qualities, but as wholes, in which the parts are arranged and organized in a relationship. The system is then the continuing state of flux in which this arrangement and organization takes place (Angyal 1969,26). This does not, however, imply an organic integration and a loss of individuality of members of the human group in the sense of the integration of cells in a biological organism. Von Bertalanffy (1969,28), in adapting his general systems theory from biological to social organisms, in fact rejects the idea of such an exact comparison between the two processes.

Another important property of systems – at any rate, open systems – looked at particularly from inside, is that they are goal-seeking, and the purpose of feedback, which we shall look at further, is to keep a system goal-directed. This characteristic of goal-seeking, and being goal-directed, is one which I have also attributed to a community.

Externally, the systems model helps us to recover some of the sense of the common living of social beings which may be thought to have been lost in turning away from the traditional concept of community toward more discrete and explicit human groupings. For the quality of interrelatedness exists not only within these groupings when they are seen as systems in themselves; it exists between such groupings and other groupings, all of them now seen as sub-systems of larger systems.

So, although in practical terms, i.e., in terms of the management of social change, it is more realistic to see community development as working through explicit organizations than through some implicit sense of social identification, systems theory enables us to relate the functioning of such discrete and explicit organizations to a wider sense of community. Indeed, systems theory *requires* people in explicit organizations to bear such a relationship in mind.

Take, for instance, a housing co-operative which operates and takes up space within a wider urban development area – situations which, in fact, exist in a new sub-division of the city of Edmonton in Alberta and in a new redevelopment area in the False Creek district of central Vancouver. The aims of the housing co-operative are directed primarily toward creating a particular life style which, in the minds of the members, embraces such values as sharing, mutual support, and economic interdependence. But the housing co-operative stands in close relationship with the rest of the development area; it shares public rights of way, green spaces, commercial facilities, schools, etc. The behaviour of the members of the co-operative and of their families therefore has to take into account the expectations of other people in the area, and the co-operative's members share with those other people certain responsibilities for the proper functioning of common facilities, and certain practices (e.g., voting for a local alderman) to ensure a minimum standard of civic government.

Loomis' concept of systemic linkage describes this relationship (1969,32). Systemic linkage is a process whereby one or more of the elements of at least two social systems are articulated in such a manner that the two systems, for some purposes and on some occasions, may be viewed as a single unit. And the elements of a social system are: the generalized set of *beliefs or knowledge*; the body of *feeling or sentiment*; the *goal* of the system; the *norms*; the *status-roles* or positions of members of the system; their *rank*; the *power base* and the kind of sanctions exercised; and the *facility* or the *means* used to attain ends within the system. While on the one hand the system has boundaries which set some limits to inter-group contact, linkages between systems allow for the interdependence of groups, which may involve one or more of the elements, such as norms, sentiment, or status-roles. The latter case exists where certain members fulfilling certain roles in one system may fulfill the same role in another system, for example, where a planner in a local government system performs a planning role as a member of a co-operative housing venture.

In the case of the housing co-operative, the boundaries between its system and the surrounding society are set at the lines where its shared values, beliefs, sentiments, and norms of conduct and of managing the co-operative's internal affairs differ from those of the people who are not in the co-operative. These distinguish the co-operative from the rest of the urban development area. But through certain common goals and shared civic responsibilities they are linked to others, some of whom – e.g., people in low-cost housing schemes in the area – may form other systems. There are, in Loomis' terms, systemic linkages.

In certain circumstances such linkages do not exist or are not strong enough, or differences between some of the elements in two systems are in strong enough conflict to negate any other linkages. In these circumstances one of the systems is likely to become an irritant and eventually an embattled enclave in an inhospitable environment. I refer later, in chapter 7, to a personal experience in Rhodesia where the multi-racial nature of a farming co-operative in a white area so offended the beliefs and norms of white society and white politicians that it was declared an illegal organization and all its property confiscated by the white regime.

When the elements which are linked are the goals of the different systems, there may be a tendency for the two systems to join and become one for certain purposes. This has happened, for instance, in the Northwest Territories of Canada, where the Indian Brotherhood and the Métis

Association have come together to oppose plans for a gas pipeline through the Territories, and have gone further to publish a joint statement declaring the existence and the rights of a Dene Nation ('Dene' being the native word for 'people'). This is an example of how community development can become part of broader political action.

But if an identity of goals is *necessary* for the merging of two or more groups or systems, it is not *sufficient*, at any rate for any stable kind of merger. For this to happen it is also necessary for there to be a sharing of beliefs, sentiments, facilities – in fact, a sharing of all the elements of each system. Without such general sharing the merger of the systems is a very unstable one and the likelihood of fission and inter-group enmity is great. This phenomenon has been seen in the past in the relationships between various communist groups, between Indian groups in North America, and between African nationalist groups in countries like Rhodesia. Sometimes the differences persist in those elements which have to do with basic beliefs, sentiments, and goals; sometimes they persist in the initiation and carrying out of action, i.e., in relation to status, role, power, and means; and sometimes they persist in all these elements. The split in the leadership of the African nationalist group in Rhodesia in 1963, which persists into the 1970s, resulted not from different goals, but partly, in the initial stages, from differences in sentiment and belief arising out of tribal identity, and mainly from notions about power, sanctions, and facility, i.e., how people in the movement should act to change the domination of the white minority. In the period leading up to the split, one sub-group led by Joshua Nkomo had taken a line that change should be induced by trying to get external governments to influence the white Rhodesian government, while another group, led by Ndabaningi Sithole, felt increasingly that change could be induced only by strong leadership and possibly by direct struggle within Rhodesia. (*Central African Examiner* 1963).

These examples bring out an important aspect of this discussion. What I am arguing in this chapter is that a community as I have defined in chapter 2 is not merely and necessarily a discrete and self-contained group in its objectives and purposes, but that it is connected to other communities in a wider social system. In the passive sense, these connections exist whether the community likes it or not. Even though it might wish to have as little as possible to do with its surrounding human environment, it shares certain common facilities and services with other communities in the social system, and people in other communities have certain expectations of its members and of itself as a collectivity. Because it will be under such observation it is likely that it will create either a negative or positive impression on them, and come to be rejected or accepted by them. If it is accepted and the outsiders' observations are favourable, it may, by example and despite its intentions, have some positive influence on the outsiders. Some of its values, e.g., of sharing, of creative communal efforts, and some of its behaviours, may be adopted by others.

There is then a continuum, from this passive stance just referred to, to a very active stance, along which a community can be connected with other communities and the wider social system of which it is a part. The nature of the connections is manifested in one or more of the elements suggested by Loomis and listed above, in other words, linkages of beliefs, sentiments, goals, norms, etc. The concept of systemic linkages, does not, however, prescribe *how* these linkages are made, and various theories of social change propose various ways in which this can happen. Moving along the passive/active continuum we might suggest these ways of creating linkages: by example (imitation by others); diffusion; the dialectic process; infiltration; colonization (political or economic); conquest.

With regard to these ways of creating linkages, community development advocates and practitioners will tend to identify themselves with the lower and middle range of the continuum, i.e., exercising influence through example, diffusion of ideas, a dialectic process, or even infiltration, but not colonization, conquest, or such aggressive and offensive strategies. But whatever strategy of influence and change is contemplated, the elements through which such influence and change will occur are those suggested by Loomis. A knowledge of those elements, and of what Loomis (1960,8) calls the structural-functional categories through which they are implements, is helpful to community development strategists.

The concept of systemic linkage is one which provides for a kind of inter-group relationship which has to do with the handling and disposition of power, and this is important because to be ultimately effective the community development process must move from a concern with learning and objective-setting to a concern with the way power is to be generated and used to influence social change. A weakness to which community development is prone, is a tendency to dwell on spiritual and moral aspects of groupness to the extent that this is seen as an end in itself, and to shy away from strategy, as if it were something which somehow carried a taint of the very condition against which community development is a countermovement. The ends of community development are political in its wide sense, and political ends are not achieved without access to, and the appropriate use of, strategy.

This has been a discussion of relationships between systems and sub-systems; it shows how elements in one sub-system can affect other sub-systems and therefore the total. And it is a feature of this analysis that it draws attention to this kind of consequential change as being of the nature of systems; change in one part of the system will yield changes in other parts. Changes in one community of people in a larger social system will bring about changes in other communities, because it will be drawing different inputs from some of those other communities and it will be producing different outputs which will impinge on them. More importantly, it will be transmitting information from itself to others, and it is this aspect of systems analysis which possibly has the greatest meaning for community development. It introduces the application of the cybernetic systems model to the relationship between people within communities and between communities as groups of people.

COMMUNICATION SYSTEMS

This brings us to a consideration of a particular variation of the systems model which is very relevant to community development: communication systems and communication models. There are two ways in which communication models can have a bearing on community development: (a) a study of the elements of the model can help us analyse the relationships within and between communities; and (b) the real technological developments which have come about in the last couple of decades as a result of advances in communication theory have actually changed the ways in which people and groups can and do relate with one another, and they therefore open up a different view of community.

The simple diagrammatic representation of a communication model is given in Figure 5.

FEEDBACK

In Figure 5, s represents the sender of a message, m represents the message that is sent, and r the receiver. For the communication to be complete there is required to be feedback from the receiver to the sender (f). Only if there is such feedback can the *intention* of the sender of the message be brought into line with the *effect* which the message has on the receiver, by a process of rephrasing or reformulating the message on the part of the sender (Wallen 1967). This concept in itself is important enough at the basic interpersonal level of group and community activity.

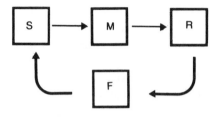

FIGURE 5 Simple communication model

Good feedback is essential for understanding between two or more persons working toward some common objective. But it goes further than that: not only is it essential for understanding; it is essential for the establishment of trust between such persons. For if the intention of the sender of a message is always different from the effect which the message has on the receiver, i.e., on the way the latter perceives what the former is getting at, then there is likely to grow between the two a lack of trust and openness, without which interpersonal communication and co-operation becomes impossible. So the model has relevance to the basic level of group effectiveness, by drawing attention to the need for good feedback in interpersonal relations.

Extending the model beyond the simple case of communication between two persons, the concept of feedback is the central element in cybernetics as applied to any working system, and particularly, for our purposes, to any social system. A fundamental theme of cybernetics is regulation and control in open systems to the end that the systems shall survive in a changing environment. Cadwallader (1969,305) points out that 'from the point of view of cybernetics, any large-scale formal social organization is a communication network.' It must contain feedback mechanisms, a certain variety of information and certain kinds of input, a channel, and storage and decision-making facilities. 'Channel' here means the medium by which information is passed into and through the system, whether it be by writing on paper, voices in the air, or complicated electronic circuitry. Information is something which moves not only within the system itself; it is an input into the system from the environment. And feedback comes to the originator of messages in the system not only from within the system but also from the environment in which the system works.

So we are dealing here with two sources of feedback, both of which are important for the functioning of the system. First is the feedback within the system. This says that in terms of how the people in the system see their goals and objectives, what is happening is or is not in accordance with these objectives. In other words, a community is formed with certain objectives, e.g., to meet certain social-emotional needs of the members and to provide them with, say, certain kinds of housing, as in the case of a housing co-operative. As the life of the co-operative progresses, members begin to express feelings that they are not happy with the way things are turning out: there is lack of privacy, or different types of housing are beginning to cause the formation of social cliques in the community. This is feedback within the system, to which it must try to react in order to prevent people from leaving it. If such feedback is provided, i.e., if members of the community can feel free to express such feelings in a forum where they are heard, then at least the community can react and adjust its affairs to meet the needs expressed, and it may achieve such an adjustment and keep itself in existence. But if such feedback is not provided, i.e., if members have no channel by which to express their feelings, then what is likely to happen is silent frustration, people moving out, and the breakdown of the community.

Feedback from outside the system may, in the case of the housing co-operative, come in a negative form of complaints from nearby residents that the state in which the housing is kept is having a bad effect on neighborhood property values, or in the positive form of comments from town planners who express admiration for the style of housing and of living which it permits, and which makes the housing co-operative the centre of studies by other urban planners. Whatever may be the feedback from the environment, it will affect the members of the system, and if it is feedback from other regulatory systems such as government, it has to be taken notice of and acted upon if the system is to survive. In some cases the feedback may come from the natural environment, in the form of the pollution of the air or the waters used by the community. An important point here is that the appropriate instruments or techniques have to be built into the system, for receiving and decoding the feedback. Social systems have to create and maintain techniques of monitoring the effects of their continuing activities, both inside and outside the system.

ENTROPY

Another related concept in communication theory which has relevance to community development is that of entropy and negative entropy. Entropy is a property of closed systems, a tendency for systems which receive no inputs from outside to run down, or lose their organization and coherence and to dissolve. In this sense, entropy could be thought of as non-community, the state of, or tendency toward, apathy and inertness. Open systems, on the other hand, can respond to the intrusion of outside influences by elaboration, adaptation, and change in their structure, which is a process of negative entropy. This in turn introduces the concept of the organized complexity of open systems, a condition where the state of the system is not simply a function of its initial formation, unchanged, but of experiences which come to it in the course of its existence. It is such a system which, on coming up against new experiences, i.e., on receiving new information or feedback from the environment, elaborates its internal structure and thus becomes increasingly complex, creating new subunits with new functions to cope with the new experiences (Buckley 1961,39).

Communication theory suggests that information coming into the system is anti-entropic or negantropic, in other words, it keeps it alert and helps prevent it from becoming stagnant. Such information can be of two kinds: feedback about the system's activities and their impact on the environment; and new information about changes that are happening in the environment independently of the system, in the form of technological change, economic change (e.g., monetary inflation), political change (e.g., new laws), or climatic change. On the basis of such feedback the open system can be innovative and can move with the times.

MEMORY

A system's memory is the store of information which it has received from outside in the past, and of its recollection of its own past experience, all of which it draws upon in confronting, or failing to confront, current experience and information which it is receiving. There are two important aspects: how the system's memory affects its internal processes, and how it affects its collective behaviour in relation to other systems.

In relation to the first aspect, the kind of questions which arise are: Where in the system does this information exist? Who holds the information? Is it held by one person, or a few, or is it spread throughout the community? How is the information selected and used to guide the decision-making of the group? These questions relate to internal power. The answers will indicate how oligarchic or democratic the system is, and practical illustrations of how it works out are available at all levels of community life.

At the international level, I used to attend, in the early 1960s, various meetings of such organizations as the General Agreement of Tariffs and Trade (GATT) and the International Telecommunications Union in Geneva, and the Commonwealth Economic Committee in London. In a sense, the people attending these meetings formed communities, insofar as they shared an identity as experts in trade, or telecommunications, or economic affairs, or whatever, and an ostensible interest in a certain order in which these matters should be governed internationally. What became apparent in such gatherings was that there were some longer-standing and larger delegations – those with many experts – who had a far better grasp than the others both of the history of previous negotiations and of current information about the subject matter in question. Consequently, many decisions were, in effect, arrived at between those delegations and followed by the others; in other words, many participants voted according to the lead of the larger delegations because they felt that they had insufficient real knowledge of the issues in question. They were unsure of themselves. This general state of affairs was sharply and ironically illustrated on one occasion during a discussion on trade boycotts at a time when boycotting South African trade was a lively issue. The lone delegate of a newly-independent African state was seated next to the South African delegation, and at one point during the debate he leaned over and said he supposed that boycotts were permitted in certain circumstances, to which a South African delegate replied firmly and with paternal assurance, 'Oh, absolutely not!'

In this connection, an interesting development at the international level is the way the Third World countries have in recent years come to re-examine their own past experience and interpret the available information, i.e., reconstruct their own memories, in such a way as to be able to confront the more developed countries, whose reconstructions of history and interpretations of information have up until recently been accepted as gospel. The result has been to make international decision-making less oligarchic – and more controversial in the developed world.

At the national level the centralizing of decision-making through the centralizing, and even the monopolizing, of information, is seen in the development in the last few years of the large and powerful inner executive team around the Canadian Prime Minister – ironically, a man who has spoken so much about participatory democracy. In the United States, Bell (1966,135-7) has described the growth of government by experts in a time when issues are so complex and involve information from so many parts of the world.

At the local neighborhood level, I have had the experience of seeing the process of decision-making being centralized in a person who came to possess the information necessary for such decisions. In the city of Edmonton, community leagues are voluntary associations of residents in areas designated by the city authorities as communities, formed to provide recreation facilities and programs in those communities with the co-operation of the city's Department of Parks and Recreation. The issue in this case was the upgrading of a playground for small children in a corner of a local park. The playground was being used increasingly by two adjacent day-care centres, which came together to request the upgrading of the playground for the use of their children as well as for general community use. This was done, as required, through the local community league. The chairman of the community league happened to be the operator of other day-care centres, more distant from the playground, and in competition with the two in question. In calling a meeting of the community league the chairman was able to make use of (a) his knowledge that only a handful of people attended such meetings, (b) information that officials of the Parks and Recreation Department had limited funds for such improvements, and (c) complaints by some residents adjacent to the playground about the noise caused in the evenings by older children. He was able to have a resolution passed at the meeting to stall the upgrading of the playground. According to the resolution, one of the conditions for possible upgrading was to be that day-care centres other than the two which had made the request be given similar facilities.

These illustrations relate to the first aspect of the question of a system's memory, i.e., how it affects the internal processes of a system. The reference to Third World nations brings out the other aspect, i.e., how the system's memory affects its collective behaviour in relation to other systems. As this group of countries re-examined history and reinterpreted available information, i.e., reconstructed its memory, it increased its ability to influence the international environment and to resist forces in that environment which had been detrimental to its members' own development. The same holds true for more localized communities. This can be illustrated in a negative way by reference to a Métis colony in the northern part of one of the Prairie provinces of Canada.

Here the community is initially defined from the outside, i.e., by the political and social forces which in the past have drawn these people together into one area. It is also defined on ethnic lines, and in this case it can be marked by certain geographical limits. In some respects it is therefore not unlike an urban ghetto community of coloured people in the United States or in a Midlands city in England.[1]

The typical Métis colony comprises a hundred or so families situated in an area some distance from main transportation routes and therefore relatively isolated. Means of livelihood are scarce or nonexistent, and most, if not all, of the families live on government welfare payments. Apathy, inertia, and even withdrawal in the form of widespread alcoholism, are evident, and the colony can be said to be an open system only in a negative sense. It is not goal-seeking, and its people adapt to the information coming from the environment in the sense only of confirming what that information tells them: that they are inferior and entirely dependent, that they are incapable of managing for themselves, that they lack the mental, organizational and technical equipment to change and improve their lot. These messages come from the government through the welfare system and through government officials in their paternalism, sometimes from the police in the way they treat the people, and frequently from white citizens in those centres with which the Métis come into contact. The feedback they receive from these sources reinforces them in their withdrawal and what is seen as anti-social behaviour.

We can say, therefore, that the memory of this community is very strong in the sense that it consists of a long accumulation of recollections of bad past experiences, and it interprets most information coming from outside in the light of those recollections. Its memory is weak in the same sense as when we refer to a person as having a weak self-image and hence tending to be very dependent, and subject to other people's influence. A weak group memory means that the community is unable to confront and challenge the information it receives from outside, so it has little ability to resist the influences contained in that information, much less to influence the surrounding environment. In an important sense, it is a non-community.

Interestingly, in this particular case, the group memory is personalized in one of its members. According to the perception of an outside observer this person is, in terms of the judgments we make about people in our society, irrational and unbalanced. He sees the world through misanthropic eyes. But he appears to be someone whose interpretation of events others in the colony seek and accept. In an important sense he is a

---

1 I am indebted for the description of the circumstances of this case to Mr Drew Lamont, a former Frontier College Community Development Officer in Canada. The interpretation is my own.

source of internal feedback to the others, providing them with assurance that theirs is the only realistic attitude toward an environment which is alien and malign. He performs the function of helping the people to reconcile their behaviour with their life situation, and he thus helps them to avoid an intolerable cognitive dissonance (Festinger 1957).

We can look at a situation such as this with reference to the discussion of development in chapter 2, where it was suggested that the early phase of community development could be seen as community creation, and where we noted four dimensions of growth; an increase in openness, i.e., in the channels of intake from the outside world; an increase in inner complementarity, or coherence; an increase in power to change the environment; and an increase in learning capacity. The brief description of this group of people in terms of the communication model may suggest some possibilities for action toward the creation of a community, i.e., the reduction of entropy, and the formulation of objectives for the group.

Looked at from inside the settlement, there is no evidence of the element of a body of information and knowledge, or a corporate myth, with which they can confront the information coming from outside. On the contrary, there is a defencelessness in the face of this incoming information. One possible strategy of community creation might therefore start by developing ways of creating or reviving a new memory.

History has not been kind to the Métis people, and they have few heroes, but there are more than we generally give credit for. Many of the famous Canadian voyageurs and coureurs de bois – those men who opened up the huge country with their canoes and snowshoes – were Métis. Louis Riel, the first challenger of the takeover of the west by the white merchant soldiers, and who in recent years has begun to be honoured rather than reviled as a figure in Canadian history, was a Métis. The point here is that the awakening of some of this kind of knowledge among such people as those who live today in Métis colonies might help toward creating a group memory with which they could confront information coming from outside. This is now beginning to happen, as it has happened among American and African Blacks, in the pride in negritude, and in the advocacy of a new history of black empires in west Africa by Kwame Nkrumah in the movement toward Ghana's independence.

But whatever such a growth of internal strength might do for the people of such settlements, they are still confronted with the information, attitudes, and actions of the outside environment. To look at this side of the matter begins to reveal some of the limitations of trying to change the condition of the group from the inside, with its own resources. Violence, such as in the Watts district of Los Angeles in the mid-1960s and in ghetto areas of many other American cities, causes more notice to be taken, a new appreciation to be formed, and ameliorating action to be initiated by governments, but violent actions are ultimate acts of frustration. Less violent action, such as the occupation by Indians of the Anicinabe Park in Kenora, northern Ontario, in 1974, may have the same effect. In Deutsch's terms, such activities certainly constitute an increase in power to change the environment, but they do not necessarily lead to an increase in openness, inner coherence, or learning capacities. The efforts of such organizations as the Métis and the Indian Associations of Alberta are directed at all four dimensions of growth, through changing the sort of information conveyed by white society to the people living within these communities, as well as building up their internal sense of self-confidence and their personal skills.

COMMUNICATION AND COMMUNITY

Meier (1962,126,144) has drawn attention to Shannon's demonstration, in the field of electronics, that inefficiency in an information system, i.e., the generation of 'noise' and the failure to exclude interference, creates a state of entropy in the system. Out of this discovery have developed techniques of automatic control and the vast improvements in electronic communications systems, which continue to take place. It has produced the giant television network, the CATV network, and the whole paraphernalia of the mass media. Means have already been created by which people spread over wide areas, urban or rural, national or international, can communicate very speedily and effectively. The barriers of communication which up until now enabled groups of people – ethnic groups or social circles, even within single cities – to live as fairly distinct social systems, have been overcome by the mass media. This has led to the ability of large organizations to impinge on the lives of people, through advertising, sponsored programs, or direct control of media, and to avoid the taint of compulsion while using manipulation and persuasion. But as Groombridge points out, it can magnify the effect of group pressures and popular manifestations by reporting them (1972).

Advance in communication technology has two effects. The first is to change the nature of communities, from being based on location to being based on communication. It necessitates a move from thinking in terms of a spatial model to thinking in terms of a communication model. Mandelbaum (1972,25) suggests that our attachment to a spatial model has been reinforced by the organization of our demographic and political life. The government census places us in a locality, and our representative institutions group us spatially for voting purposes. Communications technology has brought about such a resource of mass media, providing instantaneous information over such a wide area, as to make these spatial dimensions irrelevant. What matters in the formation of a community is the people, roles, and places with whom and with which we can communicate, and we can now do this beyond small localities. The important elements in creating a community are: a centre where intelligence or knowledge can be gathered and stored, a code in which this intelligence can be expressed and commonly understood, and a channel by which it can be transmitted both ways. This alone is not, of course, sufficient; it requires, as well, a commonly agreed purpose.

The second effect of advances in communications technology is its ability to provide for this feedback. In this respect an important instrument, particularly in densely-populated urban centres, is coaxial cable, the instrument which now makes possible the wired city. The availability of a large number of channels in one cable, and the perfection of video cameras, make practicable a system of community programming, i.e., the preparation of programs by groups of citizens about matters of public interest, which can be fed into the network and which can enable citizens and citizen groups to contribute to the formation of public policy by the airing of public sentiment. In a democratic society which enables and encourages such expressions of private or group views in a large public forum, this becomes a potentially powerful community tool. The provision of at least one community programming channel is required of all cable TV companies by the Canadian Radio and Television Commission. There are problems in this: the funding of community programs, the motivating of local people, and the organization of their efforts. But some advances have been made, particularly in the province of Alberta.

The wired city, and the wider electronically-connected society, make possible even more than this; they provide the means of instant feedback from people's homes to the centres of government decision-making, and we expect this sort of facility could be developed within relatively a few years to the point where it does in fact become an element in the political life of the more developed countries.

Such developments point to a new role for community development workers: not only of animating community groups to study matters of public concern (which role they can and do already play) but also of helping such groups to become sufficiently skilled in the uses of some of the media to be able to insert information into the public network – a process which has been called demystifying the media.

But they present a challenge to both community development workers and community groups, in a society where the established economic and political powers know of and take pains to control the power of the media and their use.

PART TWO

MODELS RELATED TO THE
COMMUNITY DEVELOPMENT PROCESS

4

Learning and community development

If learning is the first stage of the community development process, the question is: 'What is learning?' When we have learned something, what do we have? More properly, when *I* have learned something, what do *I* have? For learning is something that happens to an individual, and theories about learning are in the realm of psychology, which is concerned with individual behaviour. Community development, on the other hand, has to do with social behaviour, or the behaviour of groups of people. So what is the connection?

As a general statement, the connection lies in the following chain: learning has been defined as a change in behaviour (Gagne 1967,5; Combs and Snygg 1959,190); insofar as one behaves in a social context, i.e., in relation to other people, the behaviour has social effects; social effects become part of the social process; community development is a kind of social process that emphasizes change in relationships; in community development we are therefore concerned with individual learning that brings about, or is required for, behaviour whose effects will be a change in social relationships.

The remainder of the chapter will examine this connection further, exploring those interpretations of learning which appear to be particularly relevant to community development.

The question, 'When we have learned something, what do we have?,' points to one aspect of learning, i.e., the outcomes, or products of learning, and we can start the exploration there. It will soon become apparent, however, that we cannot neatly separate consideration of the outcomes of learning from that of the *process* of learning – how the outcomes happen. Assumptions which we make about the process affect our views about the outcomes.

A common classification of the outcomes of learning is in three forms: attitudes, skills, and knowledge. In more technical language, attitudes are synonymous with affective learning, i.e., learning that has to do with feelings and emotions. Skills, in their simplest form, are synonymous with psychomotor learning, e.g., hitting a nail with a hammer, and riding a bicycle. Knowledge is synonymous with cognitive learning, i.e., learning that has to do with cognitions, perceptions, concepts, the intellect. Values form part of both knowledge (cognitive learning) and attitudes (affective learning). The attributing of values in the cognitive domain involves judging particular ideas and objectives produced by the process of learning, according to standards of criticism internal to the idea or thing itself, i.e., consistency, logical accuracy, etc., and to external criteria related to the ends to be served (Bloom 1966,185-7). In the affective domain values relate more to generalized beliefs and to the conscience of the individual.

We can now look again at the initial stage of the community development process set out in chapter 2, where it was suggested that three sorts of learning were needed: *attitudes* toward self, others, and things: *skills* in communication and group discussion; *knowledge* of oneself, one's group, and the environment. Attitudes will consist of our emotional responses to these elements: our feelings about ourselves, i.e., self-worth and self-confidence; about people in our community, i.e., our group beliefs and traditional orientations; about people outside our group, i.e., race prejudices; and about the country-side, the city, works of art, etc. Skills, in this case, will consist of a broader range of activities than just motor skills because communication and group discussion consist not just of pure muscular movement, but the formulating of concepts and holding of certain attitudes. Knowledge will consist of our perceptions and concepts, i.e., our intellectual appreciation of people and things. What do I 'know' about myself – my skills, strengths, weaknesses; how do I perceive the skills, characters, physical attributes, of others; what do I 'know' about history, building a house, grammar, and composition?

It becomes clear in these few words that there is an intimate connection between our attitudes and our knowledge. Do I perceive myself and others in a certain way because I have certain prior feelings about them? Do I perceive things in a certain way because they are 'really' like that or because I have an inner 'gut' feeling about them? This takes us into the process of learning, and I will return to it below, after discussing the outcomes of learning a little further.

What is required in community development is a balance of learning between knowledge, attitudes, and skills. Emphasis on imparting knowledge, and ignoring or down-grading the importance of people's attitudes, is a common characteristic of specialists and professionals in development work. I have referred earlier in the book to the failure of schemes for livestock control by animal husbandry experts in Rhodesia who had no feelings about the traditions of the tribesmen. The same goes for urban development schemes initiated and carried through by planners and bureaucrats with no account of the feelings and values of those whose lives are being 'improved.' These do not exemplify community development. On the other hand, there are the justified criticisms of development workers who emphasize affective learning – feeling good – and who fail to provide people with knowledge and skills related to their needs. And a failure to help people acquire skills – even relatively simple ones such as typing, basic vehicle maintenance, or working a film projector – keeps them in a state of dependency. For different development projects or parts of projects, a different mix of learnings is appropriate.

Mogar has extended this idea of appropriate learnings to suggest that individuals showing certain tendencies in the way they learn will also tend to be especially suitable for working with people. Starting with Jungian personality theory as a basis, the process of learning is described as one of perception and of judgment. We perceive, or become aware of things, people, events, or ideas, and we then judge, or evaluate them. There are two modes of perception: sensing, i.e., relying on data received by the senses; and intuition, i.e., the internal process of seeing unconsciously the possibilities and potentialities of events, and of forming thought structures or gestalts – 'unconsciously' in the sense that a person with this tendency 'knows' without knowing why or how he knows. These two modes of perception are present in all men in varying degrees. There are, likewise, two modes of judging: thinking, i.e., relying primarily on intellectual processes for making judgments of true or false, or logical deductions and inferences; and feeling, i.e., relying on affective processes for making judgments of pleasant and unpleasant, like or dislike, acceptance or rejection. These two modes of judgment are likewise present in all men in varying degrees. But the two modes of perception and of judgment respectively are incompatible at any one time. We perceive either by sensing or intuition, and we judge either by thinking or feeling.

Mogar then goes on to suggest that individuals will tend, by and large, to fall into one of four combinations of modes of perception and judgment: sensing-thinking, sensing-feeling, intuition-thinking, and intuition-feeling. And again in broad terms of tendency, he suggests that it is the sensing-feeling person who will tend to find scope for his abilities in social service work. He/she will focus on data from outside ('facts'), will handle them with personal warmth, and will thus tend to be sociable and friendly and be interested in people (Mogar 1969,17-53).

That is one way of looking at the likely characteristics of good community development workers through learning modes, and it has led us from outcomes of learning to the process. In talking about knowledge I referred to perceptions and concepts. According to one view, perceptions are the raw impressions which we obtain through our senses, and concepts are the structures, theories and generalizations which we form from our perceptions. This is not the Jung/Mogar interpretation, as we have seen above, since perception can arise, as well, from intuition, which is some internal and unconscious mental process independent of sensations. This blurs the distinction, just referred to, between perceptions and concepts. And it is around these questions, the relationship between sense-created perceptions and concepts, and the respective importance of sensation and intuition, that arise two main schools of thought about the process of learning. I want to discuss these in their relation to community development, and to do this requires first a brief description of the main features of each school.

Allport has suggested that all modern psychological theories seem to be oriented to one of two polar conceptions, which at the risk of over-simplification can be called the Lockean and Leibnitzian traditions respectively. One, the Lockean, sees man's mind as passive in nature, an empty slate on which the outside world impinges and makes impressions, so that it is not the organism itself which is important, but what happens to the organism from outside (Allport 1955,7-9). This is, indeed, an oversimplification of Locke's ideas, which, in fact, give a very important part to intuition ('intuitive knowledge is the highest of all human activity' – Locke 1894,407), reflection, and wisdom, which is 'the product of a good natural temper, application of mind and experience together' (Locke 1963,132). Leibnitz emphasized mind as active in nature, working upon the outside world. This is a view more recently emphasized by Von Bertalanffy in his general systems theory, in which a key concept is the notion of a human organism as a spontaneous active system. 'Even under constant external conditions, and in the absence of external stimuli, the organism is not a passive but basically an active system' (Von Bertalanffy 1969,22-3).

In other words, though the main theories of the learning process fall within the area of psychology, their proponents adhere to them as much on the basis of philosophical assumptions about human nature as on scientific grounds. Data gathered in experiments, or even in less controlled situations, which in themselves are not disputed by theorists of different schools, are interpreted differently (Hilgard and Bower 1966,8). In other words, there is a difference between performance, which is an observable, measurable response, and learning, which is a non-observable, hypothetical construct which intervenes between observable variables (Spence 1959,85). Different theorists, while accepting a common body of demonstrated relationships in observed behaviour, draw different inferences from that behaviour, in accordance, one may conclude, with some predilection on their part about the nature of humanity. Looking at different theories of learning keeps in mind the different views of human nature and of man's relationship to his environment, which inform such theories. This enables us to understand, in turn, more about our own view of human nature, insofar as we find ourselves identifying with one theory more than another. Do I find myself attracted to one approach or the other? And what does this sort of attraction indicate about my assumptions about what people are like and what makes them do what they do? What does it tell me about the way I will tend to regard people and try to get them to act in relation to social problems? I have suggested in the Introduction and chapter 2 that an understanding of oneself is important for a community development worker. A knowledge of learning theories and of our reaction to the assumptions which such theories contain about human nature, may help in that understanding.

STIMULUS-RESPONSE, CONDITIONING, BEHAVIOURISM

The development of these theories – and it has been suggested, of all other theories of learning, either pro or con (Hilgard and Bower 1966, 15) – appears to stem from or react to the work of E.L. Thorndike. Thorndike's basic proposition in this regard was that animal behaviour was mediated little by ideas, but that responses were made directly to a situation, and that the same applied essentially to human beings. 'All human activity is reactivity ... Activity is not the result of a sort of spontaneous combustion; it is a response to stimulation ... Whatever action results [from the stimulus or the situation] – attention, perception, thought, feeling, glandular secretion, or muscular movement – is called the reaction or the response' (Thorndike and Gates 1930,62).

In the development of learning theory, three of Thorndike's propositions have been influential: first, the conception of connection between stimulus and response, unmediated by ideas; second, the concept of effect, or reward, as a factor in strengthening connections and the probability of repeated actions; third, the methodological emphasis on observation of behaviour, experimentation, and empiricism as a basis of theory. To follow Thorndike's path of reasoning leads to a mechanistic association between stimulus and physiological movement – avoiding any intervention of ideas, thought, motivation, drive, expectancy, reward, etc. In fact, for one member of this school, J.B. Watson, thought was no more than sub-vocal speech, the movement of muscles in the throat, in other words, a behaviour amenable to perception and measurement (Hill 1963,33). Hence the attribution to Watson of the introduction of behaviourism as a school of psychology, and the strengthening of the view that the study of psychological phenomena, including learning, must depend on the study of observable behaviour, which, as measuring devices increase in their sophistication, includes the observation of neurophysiological manifestations such as glandular secretions and brain impulses.

The most prominent and influential concept which has developed from this line of work is that of conditioning. What is called classical conditioning arises from the connection, or association, between stimulus and response. What is called operant conditioning depends on the same process, with additional emphasis on the reinforcing of the response by a reward.

This is all at the level of basic physiological reflexes, and might be thought to have little to do with learning of a more sophisticated and complex kind, e.g., at a level of feeling and thought, but once it is accepted – as Watson suggested, and as Skinner (1971,15-17) still accepts – that feeling and thought are no more than movements of the gut muscles or the chemistry of the brain, then the discussion of conditioned reflexes can be extended to cover the whole phenomenon of learning and human relationships.

In classical conditioning the reinforcement of the conditioned response happens by repetition and consolidation of the association with the stimulus. In operant conditioning, as developed by Skinner, the reinforcement of the response happens by rewarding it in a manner appropriate to the learner – pigeons rewarded with food, children rewarded with love or praise, etc.

The social aspects of learning along stimulus-response (s-r) lines have been explored further by Millar and Dollard (1964). They have examined social imitation as an explanation of the learning process, social imitation being a concept similar to that of identification in personality theory.

Basically, we identify with others, and we try to behave like them, particularly if they are what is called 'significant others' – people who have prestige and who can reward or punish us or keep rewards from us. Millar and Dollard suggest a sequence of factors in the chain of learning. First, there exists a *drive*, which is a general stimulus such as hunger or pain or cultural pressure, which makes us 'ready' to act or puts us in a set to act. Then there is a particular and direct stimulus which is called a *cue*, which directly guides the subsequent response; the cue is more likely to be responded to if it is given by a significant other. Finally, the response is *rewarded* or not. The element of drive, expressed in this way, opens out into the broader question of what other writers of the school call social variables, by which is meant that the direct and simple connection between stimulus and response proposed by Thorndike and Watson is affected by other variables, such as the characteristics of the persons who are the social models to whom the learner is exposed, the manner in which reinforcement is provided by society, and the pressure, or 'maintaining stimulus,' exercised by society in certain directions, e.g., competition, co-operation, etc. Thus history and characteristics of the learner are also factors which will influence learning. For instance, children who have built up a high dependency on others are said to show imitative behaviour more than those with low dependency (Bandura and Walters 1963,10), which is not a very original observation.

In other words, there are indications, among some writers, of a softening of the uncompromising position of Thorndike and Watson that there are no intervening ideas between an external stimulus and the object's response. However, even here the emphasis is on external conditions, making very limited allowance for internal motivation. For instance, Bandura and Walters find that their experiments 'cast considerable doubt on the utility of theories of morality which assume that self-control is mediated by a unitary, internal moral agent, such as conscience, super-ego, or sense of moral obligation' (1963,206).

Before exploring the relationships of this line of thought to community development, I wish to outline the main features of the cognitive school of learning theory.

COGNITIVE THEORIES

Whereas conditioning theory excludes consciousness (i.e., internal awareness) as a valid element in affecting behaviour, cognitive theories make consciousness a major concern of psychology. The German scholar, Wertheimer, suggested that actions should be seen as meaningful wholes – the dynamic relationship of parts that make up the whole, or what he called *gestalt*. Gestalt psychology is the main stem of cognitive learning theories. A gestalt is seen as a figure set against an undifferentiated ground, a structure. Allport (1955,27) suggested later that learning was a disposition to form such structures. It is changes which we make in the relationships between figure and ground that comprise our perception, and perception is a crucial element in thinking and learning. Understanding implies perception of a problem as an integrated whole, and not just as a matter of ascribed correctness. For example, solving an algebraic sum simply by knowing what steps to go through, but not knowing why and how the steps fit together to provide the solution, is not really understanding the sum. Rote memorization of a poem is not the same as understanding the poem.

While maintaining perception as the basis of learning, Kohler developed and emphasized Wertheimer's idea of insight, or an internal reorganization of perceptions. Kohler's well-known experiments with apes during the period of the first world war showed that these animals, provided with the means of solving a problem, were able through intuition to achieve a solution – whether by using a box to reach a banana hanging from the top of a cage, or by fitting one stick into another to reach a banana placed outside the cage. Even the activity of rats in finding the correct way through a maze could be interpreted not as a process of rewarded trial and error in the behaviourist sense but as a series of small, partial insights.

Kurt Lewin was a gestalt psychologist who developed the notions of perception with regard not so much to learning as to the wider field of social psychology, particularly motivation and personality. He did this through his concept of a life-space or field, which is the totality of 'fact' as perceived by each individual which, in turn, determines his behaviour. Learning is an expansion and reordering of one's life-space, or one's field, in one's movement toward the goals which one has set.

A further development of gestalt theory consists of linking perception with self-concept. Combs and Snygg apply field theory to learning as a process of differentiation in perception. For them 'learning is the process by which an individual is able to change his behaviour usually in some more constructive fashion, and such changes are brought about by differentiation within the perceptual field. All learning of whatever variety has as its base characteristic a progressive differentiation from a more general perceptual field' (Combs and Snygg 1959,190). Furthermore, 'learning is always a functional need. The need we are talking about is need from the behaver's point of view, not that of an outsider. Even hungry rats will not run mazes if their need to sleep is greater' (1959,194).

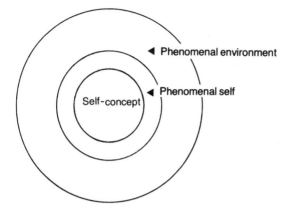

FIGURE 6 Self concept, phenomenal self, and phenomenal environment

These writers divide the perceptual field into three components: self-concept, phenomenal self, and phenomenal environment. One's self-concept is the important central perception of one's self, 'the very essence of me,' the 'self no-matter-what.' The phenomenal self is all one's perceptions of the self in a particular situation, and the phenomenal environment is all one's perceptions of oneself and of things outside oneself. Learning is, then, a process of seeing relationships among these three components (Figure 6).

A further step in the development of the role of self-concept in learning theory is suggested by Beatty and Clarke, for whom learning is 'a change in the relationship between the self and its perceived world, as the self is expressed in striving to become adequate' (Lindgren 1967,187). Hence learning is the process by which the individual becomes a fully functioning person in terms of his own capacities. This brings the individual, self concept and self-development closer yet into the centre of the whole process of learning. 'The goal of education is the production of intelligent, adequate people. The adequate personality is one who (i) perceives himself in a centrally positive way, (ii) is open to his experience or capable of accepting self and others, (iii) is strongly and broadly identified with others' (Combs and Snygg 1959,336).

It is Carl Rogers who has possibly come to represent most strongly this view of learning as a matter of personal capacity and personal growth and the ability – indeed, the necessity – of each individual to be free to make rational interpretations of his perceptions of himself and his environment. Through his experience in psychotherapy, Rogers has come to believe that learning springs from the self and that intuition is valid as a source of social as well as personal learning, because each individual has in him a microcosmic model of universal human values. 'Instead of universal values "out there," or a universal value system imposed by some group – philosophers, rulers, priests – we have the possibility of universal human value directions emerging from the experiencing of the human organism' (Rogers 1969,225). But for this to emerge requires an openness on the part of the individual to all his experience, not the suppression of it. With this openness man's behaviour 'is exquisitely rational,' whereas 'the tragedy for most of us is that our defenses keep us from being aware of rationality' (1969,291). And those defenses are built partly by the mode of learning imposed on us by the educational system.

This emphasis on values is an aspect of learning which is brought out particularly in Rogers' writing. While for Skinner, values are formulated as a response to the social contingencies created by someone in the environment – the philosophers, rulers, and priests – for Rogers 'in persons who are moving toward greater openness to their experiencing, there is an organismic commonality of value directions' (1969,251-2). Rogers goes on to suggest that openness to feelings will enable a person to learn content material, i.e., knowledge and skills, more readily.

In short, what are the main characteristics of the two schools of learning theory? For the s-r school they are: our perceptions come to us through our senses; they are caused by stimuli which are provided by someone else, either in particular or in a general way through the creation of an environment; we learn by responding to those stimuli and having our responses rewarded or punished (aversive stimuli); the reward or punishment is controlled by someone else, i.e., the ultimate choice is exercised, benevolently or not, by someone else. For the cognitive school the main characteristics are: our perceptions are generated by intuition and insights; they take the form of gestalts, or integrated structures, internally organized; the factors which influence the formation of the perceptions are internal valences, self concept, phenomenal self, phenomenal environment, and openness to all experience. Conditioning theories, therefore, tend to be more precise and more congenial to the scientific approach – more analytical – while cognitive theories make more allowance for complexity and flexibility in our intellectual processes – more synthetical.

RELATIONSHIP TO COMMUNITY DEVELOPMENT

Having sketched the main features of the two approaches to learning I want to suggest some ways in which these approaches are relevant and appropriate to community development, as models of a process (of learning) which is central to its philosophy and practice.

In the preface I have suggested that community development rests on certain underlying propositions; that people are capable of perceiving and judging the condition of their lives; that they have the will and capacity to plan together in accordance with these judgments to change that condition for the better; that they can act together in accordance with these plans; and that such a process can be seen in terms of certain values. These propositions reflect a general view as illustrated in the definitions in appendix A. What they amount to is a view of man as an active agent in his world, not a passive receiver of stimuli which, in conjunction with certain rewards, direct him. This stance therefore suggests a congruence between community development and the cognitive theories of learning, in that both take the same general view of people's capacities.

This is important; both speak to the question of man's potential. They sustain the distinction suggested by Giorgi (1975) between humans and other living creatures: 'the ability of man to overturn any given structure in which he finds himself, his symbolic power, and his power to reflect on his own lived experience.' Supporters of community development do not deny that socialization does occur, that the dominant mode in most formal education systems follows the s-r line, that despite modern management theory the dominant management practice is still one of reward and punishment. Against these realities, to hold to the view of man inherent in the cognitive model of learning, and to make it a part of the armoury of community development, might be considered idealistic, even naive. But if there is such an element of idealism in community development, there is also an element of protest, and an advocacy of alternative (and often subversive) ways of learning and development. Such protest, when activated by people like Freire in communities in Brazil, come to be seen as revolutionary on the one side, as liberation from the controllers on the other (Freire 1972).

Freire's work in Brazil, and that of his followers in Chile until the overthrow of the Allende regime, are examples of the implementation of the cognitive learning model as part of a strategy of development. Expressed in literary terms, we have *Walden Two* as a statement of the political implications of Skinner's s-r model (1962), and Walden Two is only a perfected model of what is a common political reality, at both community and national levels. 'Isn't it true that your Planners and Managers exercise a sort of control which is denied to the common members?' 'But only because that control is necessary for the proper functioning of the community' (Skinner 1962,233).

Those sentiments are not out of this world.

To bring the discussion nearer to our common experience we can consider some of the main strategies of development as they have been described by various writers, in the light of the two schools of learning theory. Earlier in this chapter I suggested that the cases of a livestock control scheme and urban development schemes planned by experts and carried through by local government authorities, were not examples of community development. They were a form of social engineering. They were such not only because they ignored the affective side of learning. The 'aversive stimuli' applied to those who did not behave in appropriately accepting fashion – in the one case, fines and 'reallocation' to other areas, and in the other, eviction or the condemning of property – were within the spirit and letter of conditioning theory.

Strategies of development have been variously categorized in the literature of social change. Starting with a broad and relatively simple categorization, the typologies have become more complex, as can be illustrated by the following list of authors and their typologies:

POWELL AND BENNE 1960
1 Developmental strategies: – an experiential involvement of the people concerned, in planning and organizing the change process.
2 Rationalistic strategies: traditional, didactic 'liberal' education, based on the premise that people can be guided by reason and information

CHIN AND BENNE 1969
1 Empirical-rational: like the rationalistic perspective listed above.
2 Normative-re-educative: people assumed to be active in their development, fitting environmental resources to their self-experienced needs. Like the developmental perspective listed above.
3 Power-coercive: the use of economic and political sanctions, and sometimes moral suasion, in the exercise of power.

DEVELOPMENT ASSOCIATES 1976
1 Cultural development: a basic questioning of the dominant culture and an

assertion and development of the values and identity of the group in question – usually ethnic in character.

2 Social-political action: involvement of groups of citizens in social and/or political action to acquire power to confront existing structures with a view to changing them.

3 Community development: citizen participation in goal-setting and problem-solving, tending not to go as far as confrontation for immediate structural change.

4 Social planning: reliance on professionals and expert knowledge to guide and support citizen involvement.

5 Information-communication-education: similar to Powell and Benne's rationalistic strategy, with the source of information apart from the citizens, to bring about controlled change.

The first two of these typologies suggests something about the approach of adult educationalists to community development. In the first one Powell and Benne, writing in the context of adult education, suggest two strategies of development which assume a capacity, on the part of those involved in the process, to take a critical look at information, to weigh it up, and to act on it in ways useful to them. In the second, rationalistic, strategy there is an acceptance of the lack of a need for affective involvement, and that rational, intellectual learning will be enough to persuade a person to change behaviour. There is not yet, however, an explicitly reward/punishment element in the process.[1] In other words, dominant in adult education is the cognitive learning model. This is expressed by Miller, writing about teaching and learning in adult education: '... there is strong evidence for believing that the kind of learning that is described by the stimulus-response model occurs at the early stages of human development, but that at the higher levels we must shift gears and adopt an explanation which is distinctly closer to the cognitive model' (Miller 1964,38).

Later, however, when Benne and Chin are examining development strategies over a broader range, they acknowledge a type of strategy involving coercion and sanctions, which reflects the conditioning approach to learning.

1 It is interesting to read, in this connection, Bertrand Russell's description of how for many years he, too, believed that the way to persuade people to change their behaviour with regard to such issues as disarmament and the outlawing of nuclear weaponry was by presenting them with reasoned, intellectually sound argument and information, as he did in many books, articles, and speeches in the 1940s and 1950s. At length, however, he perceived this to be a futile exercise and involved himself with social action groups, for which he suffered imprisonment (Russell 1971,chap. 3).

The Development Associates typology was formulated as the result of a recent survey of thirty development projects across Canada. In the choice of these projects, out of the hundreds initially considered, there was an elimination of projects which were clearly welfare delivery services, run, controlled, and financed by government or other agencies. Such programs – for example, social assistance schemes, and overnight shelters and settlement houses in ghetto areas – showed clear features of control, and of reinforcement or punishment of those who come within their orbit and accept or transgress the conditions laid down. The workers in such services commonly behave like Skinner's planners and managers, not as community development workers.

But even among those programs which were initially judged to show some features of community development – i.e., that they should involve people and encourage participation in planning, decision-making, and implementation, and should show evidence of learning as part of the development goal – some revealed strong elements of the control and reward/punishment approach of conditioning learning theory. In one Toronto program, for instance, a local grass roots social action scheme, funds were cut off by city and provincial sources and business interests after four years of increasing success in community organizing. Similarly, in Alberta a government program involving community development field workers financed under a centralized Human Resources Development Authority succeeded in mobilizing local people's energy in a number of northern communities and giving them a good deal of initiative, only to have tighter controls imposed on the community development field worker, and eventually the Authority closed down. In other words, too different attitudes toward social development were revealed: among the local workers an espousal of the view of people's capacities congruent with the cognitive learning model, and among the bureaucrats – or enough bureaucrats to matter – an espousal of the view of control congruent with the conditioning learning model.

In general, what was indicated in the Development Associates study in Canada was that those projects which were seen as falling into the categories of cultural development, social-political action, and community development, displayed a belief in the active and self-directed nature of people. But time and opportunity has to be given to people to realize this for themselves, particularly those whose long experience has been to be directed and controlled. And since this is a common experience, the process of community development takes time and patience. It is as if, having been subjected as children to a long regime of education in the conditioning mode, we find it difficult to appreciate and realize our own growing maturity. But as Miller suggests, this does come about.

There is, however, even at the adult level, one feature of the s-r model which seems appropriate to community development and that is that people's learning can be judged only by their observable behaviour. In social affairs an insistence that learning and development is something internal and ineffable raises the difficulty of assessing when and to what extent development has taken place. I will return to this point in chapter 9, which deals with evaluation in community development.

Cognitive learning theory does not reject the notion, which conditioning theory emphasizes, that our environment influences our learning. The environment is the phenomenal field, a part of the life-space, in which our perceptions are formed, and in which we act. In the next chapter I discuss the way in which, in the process of moving from learning to social action, we may make sense of that environment. It involves what Freire calls the 'decoding stage' of the development process, the early stage of consciousness-raising among people whose shared condition gives them a community of interests, and who, in Freire's philosophy, have the capacity to 'name their world' (Freire, 1970).

In chapter 6, I return briefly to this discussion of models of learning and their underlying assumptions about the nature of man and social behaviour, to lead into a discussion of the way people learn and behave in groups, and thereby begin the action stage of the community development process.

5

Environment and culture

The model of the community development process in chapter 2 suggests that the process starts with a state of tension arising out of some problem or some goal that has to do with the quality of life. Most of these tensions arise from relationships between people, institutions and the physical environment; they are the result of forces engendered by these relationships. To understand these tensions – which is the first step toward releasing them – we need to be able to identify and make sense of the elements in the environment which bear on the problem. In other words, we need a model for analysing and learning about the environment.

In this chapter I outline two such models. The first is formulated from my own experience and is relevant to program planning in both adult education and community development. I have elsewhere described a variation of this model with reference to comparative studies in lifelong education in different societies (Roberts 1973).

The second model comes out of a particular context, the reestablishment by the Indian people of Alberta of a cultural base for their life in today's world, but it has a wide relevance as an example of an analysis that emphasizes the heart and feelings of people, elements which are very much part of the general counter-cultural and consciousness approach to change and which are particularly relevant to a minority group seeking to rebuild its identity.

What both models do – since they are about the analysis of the social environment – is to raise again the question of paradigms within which social change is viewed.

MODEL I

This model directs attention to five elements to be looked at in seeking to

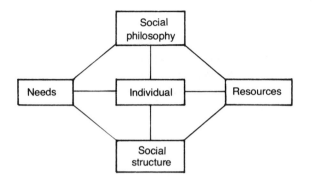

FIGURE 7 Elements in the environment of community development

understand the context in which a community development process takes place (Figure 7).

The first four elements are related to the social collectivity. They are: the social philosophy, the social structure, the needs, and the resources. The fifth element in the model, the individual, brings into question the relationship between the individual and the collectivity. This relationship – the place accorded to the individual in the scheme of things – will be reflected in the nature of, and the relationships between, the other elements. In community development terms, the opportunities available to the members of the society to develop themselves and initiate or participate in changes in the society are influenced by the prevailing social philosophy and social structure. The main elements of the social structure, that is the political, economic, and other institutions, suggest the need for certain kinds of knowledge and skills, and provide the resources for learning them. The relationship between social philosophy and social structure influences the way people learn about their environment, the content of their learning, the resources available to them. The social structure, in other words, reflects the ends which the social philosophy sets out for the society and its members, and it creates the structural context in which learning takes place.

Social philosophy – values and paradigms
By social philosophy I mean the main political and social ideas which are inherent in the behaviour of those people and groups in society who exercise power and enjoy authority. I use the term 'inherent in' because as is sometimes the case with organizations, the professed goals are not in fact those which are being pursued; organization theory calls this 'goal dis-

placement' (Etzioni 1964,10-12). The goals are sometimes set out explicitly, as in President Nyerere's statement of the 'National ethic' in his Arusha Declaration and 'Education for self-reliance' in Tanzania. Sometimes they are expressed not in single statements but in a variety of places such as Presidential speeches, speeches from the throne, budget speeches, or development plans, or they may be only explicit in policy and planning.

What social philosophy is about is the relationship between the individual and society. We are concerned with two things: hypotheses about people and hypotheses about forms of government. By hypotheses about people I mean assumptions about people's capacity to make responsible choices and to grow – what Maslow calls self-actualization. By hypotheses about forms of government I mean assumptions about the kind of political regime best suited to permit and encourage self-actualization. Such expressions of democracy place the emphasis on the individual vis-à-vis the formal social and political units and society as a whole, in what may be considered a typically western democratic way. And historically community development has derived its main impetus from British and American administrators and social scientists and has found its main expression among British and American writers. There are, however, reasons to resist simply identifying community development with the kind of political forms that exist in these countries. Even in these countries there exist power relationships at the national level which call in doubt the efficacy of what is termed community development, and particularly that aspect of community development which suggests or implies that effective local community action against inequality of opportunity can be integrated into wider national action, as suggested in the United Nations definition (see appendix A) (Marris and Rein 1967,164-90; Hill and Isaacharoff 1971,260).

Another way of looking at this is to pose some of the features of community development, such as the democratic process, community participation, the meeting of grass roots needs, and the value of the person, in the context of other kinds of regime, such as those in China and Tanzania. In both these countries the term 'democracy' is used to describe the process of government. Though Mao Tse-Tung writes of the need to ensure democracy under centralized guidance (Mao 1972,116), he repeatedly affirms such views as 'the right task, policy and style of work invariably conform with the demands of the masses at a given time and place' (Mao 1972,123), while his admonition that one must act in accordance with the needs and wishes of the masses might have been taken straight from the western manual on community development (ibid., 124). And the interpretation of Chinese life under communism at the village level by William Hinton, and at a more poetic level by Alberto Moravia, would seem to support a proposition that both at the level of local social action and at the level of hypotheses about people, community development could be said to be happening in China. These interpretations are supported by my own observations of decision-making at the commune and county level in China, during visits in 1975 and 1978. Moravia (1969,80), for instance, perceived 'the whole man of peasant society' as he went about China, and 'the humanly intact man that one can observe today in the streets of Peking' (ibid., 81), while Hinton's description of a ke t'sao, a technique of public report and appraisal in the village of Long Bow in the early days of consolidation of the Communist party in 1948, which he compares with an American 'buzz-session,' could be used in a workshop for community development trainees in Canada or anywhere else as a good illustration of group involvement and decision-making (Hinton 1968,277-8).

Likewise, in Tanzania the Arusha Declaration of Nyerere and the ruling TANU party is anchored in the concept and practice of democracy and the inherent dignity of the individual in accordance with the Universal Declaration of Human Rights (TANU 1967). Ujamaa is an expression of local co-operative decision-making about life at the local community level, even though this happens within broad policy lines set out at the national level. It can be thought of as being democracy at the grass roots. From the individual through to the nation the key concepts are self-reliance and co-operation. 'If every individual is self-reliant the Ten-house cell will be self-reliant; if all the cells are self-reliant the District will be self-reliant. If the Districts are self-reliant, then the Region is self-reliant, and if the Regions are self-reliant, then the whole Nation is self-reliant and this is our aim' (TANU 1967,18).

These brief references to China and Tanzania are not sufficient, and are not meant, to substantiate firm conclusions about community development in these countries. It is possible to argue that the tolerance, and even the encouragement, of local planning, development and achievement, is greater in China than it is in Canada and the United States. It is an even clearer possibility that the ultimate goals or value systems to which community development contributes, may be entertained in political regimes which differ from Western democracy. In other words, these goals should be seen in terms not of certain specific political regimes but of assumptions about people and of local collective life. The cultural norms of China and Tanzania which underpin the political practicalities of Maoism and of the type of African socialism being attempted by Nyerere, place the individual in a more subordinate position to society than in the west, and they allow for no completely autonomous person. One is a citizen, then an individual, and it is the corporate nature of life through which the individual fulfills himself. Moravia suggests that the essence of the difference between the view of the nature of man in relation to society in China and in western Christian cultures is indicated in the Christian concept of *sin*, wherein a man transgresses in relation to himself, as a private being, and the Chinese concept of *shame*, wherein a man transgresses in relation to others as a social being. Man's virtue in the west is personal and individual, in China it is civic, political, and social (Moravia 1969,93). Although, as with most neat aphorisms, this is an over-simplification of cultural complexities, it illustrates the possibility of different political contexts in which man may fulfill his nature.

The emphasis in community development as seen from the western point of view tends to be on what Biddle calls his summary operational assumption, namely, a patent belief in the good of people in their tendency to develop themselves into more ethically competent persons as a result of their involvement in the *self-guided* process (my italics) (Biddle and Biddle 1966,72). Others might put it thus: a patent belief in the good of people and in their tendency to develop into more ethically competent persons as a result of their involvement in the *socially-guided* process. Goodness and the development of ethical competence are, in both, the core beliefs. The social instrumentalities differ.

With these kinds of distinctions in mind we can formulate a typology of social philosophies against which we can view possible goals and strategies – or even the feasibility – of community development. It would arise out of two questions.

1 Is it the assumption that all the people in the community should learn to the best of their faculties how to take part in the exercise of power and authority in the society, or that the majority should learn to accept the assumption of authority by the few? – I.e., an equalitarian or an élitist education (Anderson 1961-2).

2 Is it the assumption that people should accept the exercise of power for the benefit of the collectivity as a whole, or expect the maximum freedom to act as individuals?

These questions refer to two sets of dimensions: the democratic/authoritarian dimension and the individualist/collectivist dimension. The second question implies a clear distinction between individualism and collectivism, but in practice there is a blurring of the distinction in a sort of middle ground which can be called pluralism. So the typology can be expressed in diagrammatic form as shown in Figure 8.

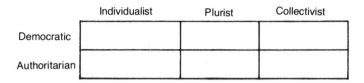

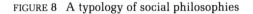

FIGURE 8 A typology of social philosophies

Along the one dimension, 'democratic' denotes a condition in which broad political, social, and economic policies are determined by a process which genuinely attempts to engage the general public and is subject, at least periodically, to public vote. 'Authoritarian' denotes a condition in which such policies are determined by one person or an oligarchy not answerable to the general public. Along the other dimensions, 'individualist' denotes a condition in which the unit of reference and of benefit is the individual, with maximum individual freedom. 'Pluralist' denotes a condition in which the unit of reference and of benefit is a variety of groups identified in some way, e.g., economic interests, as Woolf (1965,39) suggests is the case in the United States, or racial groups, as in South Africa. 'Collectivist' denotes a condition in which the unit of reference and of benefit is the society as a whole, or the state.

So, although some might suggest that Canada represents a society with a democratic/individualist philosophy, it is probably truer to identify it as democratic/pluralist. Russia could be described as having an authoritarian/collectivist philosophy, and white South Africa an authoritarian/pluralist philosophy. The important thing is not to try to fit every country or society *a priori* into these types, but to try to relate the possibilities for community development to a perceived social philosophy, after forming such a perception in the environment itself. One fault in some social analyses and some community development policies in developing countries is that they have been carried out by visiting experts in terms of assumptions held, and possibly valid, in the expert's home country, without sufficient regard to the conditions in the developing country (Simey 1968,131).

Social philosophy and social structure
I suggested above that the relationship between social philosophy and social structure affects opportunities for human development. One can use the example of the United States to examine this briefly.

Much of the literature on American education today is aimed at demonstrating the divergence between the professed social ideals of freedom, equality of choice, etc., of the United States and the real purposes which the American education system seems to serve, i.e., the ideas inherent in the behaviour of the people in those orders of the society which exert power. For example, Derbyshire (1966) has described how the realization of what is held to be a common set of values of success, progress, freedom, equality, in the United States is outside the experience of many Americans. Cicourel and Kitsuse (1963) reveal the American school as a mechanism of social differentiation.

It is sometimes only by making a close study of the actual institutional structure and the way it operates – the effects which it produces, as shown in a study such as that by Cicourel and Kitsuse – that one can understand the real as distinct from the professed philosophy and goals of the system. It is the same kind of question as that referred to by Etzioni when he discusses the difference between what the top executives state to be the goals of an organization and what is observed to be happening in the organization in terms of actions and relationships between its members (Etzioni 1964,6-7). In the language of systems theory, to discern the *function*, i.e., what actually goes on, gives us a clearer knowledge of the *goal*. A society may have a declared social policy of equal opportunity for all people, while the social structure, including the educational system, may indicate that some form of élitism is the actual objective. So, the next step in working through this model, after trying to discern the basic social philosophy, is to examine the social structure.

Social structure

By social structure I mean the complex of existing institutions and their roles in shaping the lives of the people in the society. The formal institutions are complemented, and sometimes contradicted, by informal institutions. The literature about community and business organizations is rich in cases of the informal organization working against, or protecting people from the pressures of, the formal organization, among the best known examples of this being Whyte's (1943) street corner society and Mayo's Hawthorne studies (1960).

Diagrammatically, one might depict the social structure in terms of the existing institutions as shown in Figure 9. We have to take into account not only the social structure as it seems to exist, i.e., the existing institutions and the relationships between them, but the changes in these institutions and the relationships between them. And in most countries, whether more or less developed in the economic sense, the shift between rural and urban populations, and the effects it has on both rural and urban institutions, is one of the most important phenomena of social change.

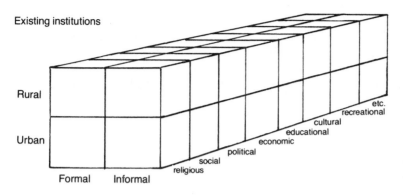

FIGURE 9 Social structure

One way in which institutions affect the direction and pattern of development is through their informal influence on people in their daily lives.
One of the most obvious of these is the influence of economic institutions
on human perceptions and behaviour through advertising, which is enor-
mously increased by the mass media and world-wide communication systems. This particular question is part of the much more general and pro-
found one relating to the effects of capitalist economic development not
only on Third World countries, but also on basic mental attitudes of dependence among the people in 'developed' countries. How, for instance,
does the administration of social assistance to poor people tend to make
them see themselves? What estimate of themselves does it persuade them
to adopt? How do public housing programs and the kind of housing provided, and its locality, affect people's perceptions of themselves? How is
status allocated – according to money, birth, occupation? How do competitive games and team games influence the notion that people have of themselves and of their social values? All these perceptions and modes of behaviour are both a result and a reinforcement of a process of learning which
affects people's capacity to take social action. One of the functions of a
community development worker is to get people to be aware of these influences, because these informal – sometimes called 'accidental' – forms of
learning tend to be overlooked; learning is too commonly seen solely in the
context of the education system. One of the important questions to be asked
with regard to institutions in the social structure is: Which ones have
power? And where, in the institution, does the power lie?
   I emphasize learning and education not only because it is the direction
from which I have come into community development, but because of the

intimate relationship between education and development. Stensland (1976) points out the present preoccupation of educationists with development by citing the number of discussions on the subject appearing in the major education journals from two major American universities, Columbia and Harvard. He goes on to point out that a central aspect of development actions, whether local, regional, national, or global, is purposeful learning, and that a great deal of such learning happens in non-formal and non-traditional settings.

Needs

In discussing needs, one useful distinction to be made initially is between expressed, or 'felt' needs – to use a term common in community development parlance – and latent needs. Who 'feels' or expresses the need – the people themselves, or the community development worker, or some visiting expert? By whose system of values do we judge that needs are latent and simply have to be teased out? One tendency in applying an economic model of development is to impose on to people in one society the economic needs expressed in another society – those needs represented by the economic term 'effective demand.' It is a main point in Ivan Illich's argument that much of the effort of external investment in the development of poorer countries of the Third World goes into creating effective demands for the sophisticated production and consumption of goods of the highly industrialized countries (Illich 1970,60). Thus 'latent' needs become 'felt.' It is an axiom in community development that such a jump is a negation of the community development philosophy, and a crucial element in this philosophy is that the people must be permitted, even encouraged, to develop, no matter how gradually, their own awareness of what it is that they need. But it is a common experience and practice that under pressure of government or other agency administrations, and the tendency of such administrations to require signs of action, needs are assumed and programs are started to meet them.

But there is also an opposite danger. There is a great deal of truth in Erasmus' (1968) contention that there exists among many community development workers a high-mindedness which tends to ignore some of the hard economic factors in development, as well as the wants expressed by people in developing countries for the kinds of consumer goods that appear to characterize 'advanced' societies – the transistor sets which so many Africans love to acquire and carry around with them, the bicycles, the cars, the TV sets, etc. And high-mindedness about the corrupting influence of these goods can become a presumption about what is really good for the citizens for these societies. It can then become paternalism, and then irritation and frustration at the inability of these citizens to make the right choices, and then a lapse into authoritarianism. This leads back to Illich's questioning of the type and direction of education that is exported to developing countries and which, Illich suggests, does not help people make the right choices for themselves and their countries, but builds up the same expectations as those in countries whose economies can easily provide sophisticated products.

With these comments in mind, there is an element of presumption in proceeding to suggest, within the framework of an analytical model, the kinds of developmental needs which will reveal themselves in any particular study, but it may nonetheless be helpful to suggest some categories of need which should be borne in mind. And these categories are: social, cultural, psychological, political, economic, and educational.

By *social needs* are meant those which arise from social changes such as movements of population from rural to urban life; from changing family relationships such as a decline of the extended family and the emergence of the nuclear family; from the increasing mobility of people in terms of both occupation and geography; from changes in age distribution in the population; from longer life in retirement. These phenomena, and the needs they give rise to, will clearly differ in different societies, and their discovery requires an existential study of the particular environment.

Cultural needs might well be classified with social needs. They arise especially out of the meeting of different cultures, and tensions between traditional and industrial (or industrial and electronic) society – the strains which are placed on groups in transition from one culture to another. To what extent is an effort being made, for instance, deliberately to foster the continuance or revival of traditional customs and mores of different ethnic groups? To what extent is such an effort being demanded by such groups as the Canadian Indians? On the other hand, to what extent is the emphasis the other way around, i.e., the moulding of people from different traditions and cultures into a homogeneous society, as was the aim of so much adult education in the United States in the early decades of this century? What needs arise among, for instance, the Eskimo and Indian people in the Canadian north, as oil drilling proceeds and oil pipelines are built? Cultural needs of these sorts lead to the possibility of counter-cultural strategies of change being adopted by the affected communities (Crowfoot and Chesler 1974).

Psychological needs are the needs of the individual himself in coping with the disorientation and alienation brought about by these other changes. They include, these days, and in some societies, needs arising out of what has been called existential neurosis – coping with the meaning of existence in a condition of shifting values and the discounting of faith.

By *political needs* is meant, for community development purposes, needs for education and training to help people take a part in the government process, initially at the local level. They are the needs highlighted under the current apparent enthusiasm for participatory democracy. And these needs, from experience in Canada and Africa, arise in relatively industrialized and 'developed' countries as well as in the developing countries. Here again, what is at issue is the needs that reveal an existing lack of power to influence public decisions.

By *economic needs* I mean those relating to education and training for occupations, at all levels of skill: labour and management training and consumer education to help people make more rational choices in the face of marketing strategies of producers and distributors. It is the first of these, subsumed under the term, 'manpower development,' which tends to be paramount in development plans sponsored by international development agencies and in plans for increased adult education in relatively developed areas such as the Canadian provinces.

Finally, I include *education needs* having particularly in mind the education of adults, upon whom the burden of community development mainly falls. The needs of adults depend so much on what kind of education is available to them as children. This is illustrated by the fact that adult literacy programs, and adult education in general, are given much higher priority in community development programs in developing countries with a relatively small proportion of school-going children and a legacy of poor educational provision in the colonial past, than in more developed countries with a wide basis of education in early years. It is also illustrated in the history of the working class movement in Britain, in the fire and energy of the Workers Education Association in the early years of this century when secondary, and even elementary education, were limited.

The implication of all this is that in the broad sense development is integrally bound into education at the earlier, pre-adult level, as well. Inequality of educational opportunity, and the assimilation of the young into the value system and social structure of existing holders of power, are themselves indicators of needs for social change. 'Societies must be prepared to consider the lessening of disparities as a major political, social and educational goal' (OECD, quoted by Stensland 1976).

Resources

When we come to try to analyse and quantify the resources available for development in any region we run into some difficulty. First, resources and needs can be difficult to distinguish neatly from each other. They are often obverse sides of the same condition. A need is often a lack of a resource – the social dimension of Maslow's notion of personal deficiency needs and growth needs.

Following from this, the same kind of comment has to be made about resources as about needs. There is a danger of assuming that what are deemed to be resources in some societies are requirements for development in others. For instance, the reliance of western education on elaborate schools and teachers trained and certified in certain institutions may cause a western observer to conclude, on looking around a developing country, that because such resources of college or university trained teachers and of well-equipped schools do not exist in large numbers, then education programs cannot be initiated. Again, Illich's point, and Freire's (1972,chap. 2), is that the resources of education are there, among the people themselves, but they can be realized only if they are recognized. Even in the literature of more economically advanced societies, the existence of educational resources among people outside the educational institutions is now being increasingly recognized (Alberta 1972,241-3).

There is another way in which the conventional views of what are needs and what are resources should be re-examined. There remains in industrial societies a strong view that resources of manpower for jobs needing some skill – commonly called the trades – are measured by the number of people who have been through an apprenticeship of anything up to five years. This view gets a good deal of its support from trade unions. But it has been demonstrated that adequate work in many operative and technical jobs in industry can be performed by persons with low basic education and with periods of only a few months of training of a special – and not necessarily expensive – kind. I have, myself, observed this process and its application in a scheme operated by Philips, the Dutch electrical firm, in Rhodesia in the early 1960s in the training of African radio repair technicians. The process follows lines developed in the second world war in Britain for the rapid training of women to work in textile and armament factories.

The point of this is to indicate that we should not accept automatically, in situations where development is an important aim, the conventional judgment of what are resources and what are not. Just as with needs, there are many latent resources in any group of people.

Having said that, an examination of these resources in any situation can be directed at three groupings: human, material, and organizational resources. But one more general comment should be made. The study of resources available to a group of people wishing to change their condition of life moves the analytical and learning stage of the process of community development towards the action stage, and the study of resources has to be thorough in order to maximize the chance of success of any action.

By *human resources* I mean, on the one hand, the numbers and the skills of people who can (a) do things and (b) help others to learn to do things. The latter include not only teachers within the formal education system, or trainers in other fields, but also community members with various abilities. Whereas the resources in the form of trained teachers are fairly easily identifiable, the others are less so. They exist in many organizations and in government departments, and many of the latter are available as resources for training citizens in such skills as organization and leadership. For instance, in the Province of Alberta, Canada, there are at least eight different provincial ministries (let alone federal government ones) which offer some form of service of this nature through people with a whole variety of skills, such as teachers, public health nurses, youth workers, and 'human resource development consultants.' Lowe (1970), in his introduction to *Adult Education and Nation Building*, points to the variety of resources in adult education and community service.

Another less tangible element of human resources is the cultural tradition which various societies have with regard to progress and success, i.e., their system of values, which may well differ from those represented by the work ethic and material wealth. This is the obverse of social and cultural needs. By what standards are we to judge that needs exist, and that resources are available to meet such needs? As I have suggested above, both needs and resources have to be judged in the light of the particular society and its aims and values, and not of those assumed by an outside observer.

Material resources can be considered under three sub-headings: financial, physical, and natural.

Since the financial resources of most groups which become involved in community development are minimal – and their lack is often seen as being one of the chief problems facing the group – the common view is that outside sources of funds have to be sought. It is here that what starts off by being a study and analysis of the forces in the environment in which the group exists becomes a plan of action. In other words, a tendency to see problems of social change and of power in terms of financial resources and a control over such resources, can obscure other issues, blind people to other resources, cause groups to come to premature conclusions about courses of action, and lead to outcomes which leave the original tensions as great as ever.

Physical and natural resources fit together, if physical resources are taken to be those that are constructed (buildings and means of communication), and natural resources are taken as the geographical resources of nature (climate and terrain). For instance, the availability of a building as a meeting place is pretty well essential for the organization of any local effort by an Indian group during most of the year in Northern Canada, while for much of the year no such enclosed place is necessary for a group in tropical Africa. Likewise, it is possible to argue that the folk school movement in Denmark, which has made a mark on Danish life, owed something to the natural phenomenon of the fallow winter period, during which country people could leave their farms for periods of learning in the folk schools. It is possibly easier to recognize as a resource the availability of soil, climatic conditions, and markets which allow the seasonal cultivation of cash crops, which in turn allow the cultivators sufficient security to be able to turn to programs of social change in the off-season. And finally, greatly improved means of communication enable groups spread over much greater distances than the traditional horseback ride or walking distance, to make and keep contact and concert their development plans.

Finally, organizational resources represent the amalgamated effort of human resources – including the presence of a tradition of voluntary work – and the other resources. They are the means by which separate individuals come together to put themselves in a position of power to influence others. They also reflect the social philosophy and the social structure of the society, e.g., tendencies toward centralized control or local autonomy, in government and voluntary efforts. A marked element in developing countries which are still emerging from the colonial past is that organizations and organizational skills have to be force-fed, because of a limited pool of trained local people and because foreign influences in the form of outside experts employed on contract (e.g., in the former French-African countries), or of foreign companies on which the economy is heavily dependent (e.g., the copper companies in Zambia) may affect existing types and patterns of organization and the existence of sophisticated organizational skills among the indigenous people.

The availability or not of organizational skills and of the kinds of local organizations in which they can be used, such as festival committees, women's associations, farmer's groups, and trade unions, has two effects. First, it affects the ability of groups to get together and work together, and second, it affects the willingness of outside sources of financial assistance to put money into new community efforts. This goes equally for dispensers of finance in north American cities such as United Community Funds, and for foundations, trusts, and governments in developing countries. It is for these reasons that much of the early effort in community education goes into leadership and organizational training.

The individual
In the middle of it all it is the individual, from whom stems a need and who can be a resource. The extent to which he can influence the social philosophy and social structure, and to which it is he, and not the collectivity, who is the central point of reference in the developmental scheme of things, is an important factor in distinguishing between different environments and different strategies of change. The needs of people will have some influence both on the social philosophy and on the kinds of institutions which emerge through time. And the people, both in the initial needs which they express as members of society and in the changing needs which they acquire as they develop – that is, their rising level of aspirations – will influence all the other four elements in the model.

MODEL II

The first model exemplifies a rational, orderly, systematic and purposeful approach to the analysis of an environment. The process of narrowing down the focus from the broad social philosophy to the social structure and then to the needs and resources, becomes a process of identifying feasible courses of action. For needs and resources are not only elements in the environment; they are elements in the population which are concerned with change, and they can therefore become identified as factors in the process of planning and organization. This analytical approach therefore fits well with the perspective of social change which Crowfoot and Chesler (1974) call the political perspective, i.e., rational and deliberate planning combined with political action.

The next model has characteristics of what Crowfoot and Chesler call the counter-cultural perspective, which emphasizes the symbolism and inner identity of cultures and sees change in terms of consciousness.

Over the last decade the Indian people of Canada have begun to articulate and implement their resistance to the exploitation they have suffered over the last century. They have looked more closely at their present condition – widespread poverty, alcoholism, poor housing, poor education, family breakdown, etc. – have sought to understand the causes of this, and have acted to improve it.

One form of action is the adoption of the political processes and practices of the white world, i.e., the formation of associations with broad political aims; the learning and practising of skills of organization, negotiation, and lobbying; the careful analysis and the use of existing laws and legal instruments (the Indian Act and the treaties) to their advantage; in other words, playing the white man's game as well as the whites do. The Indian Association of Alberta under its young president, Harold Cardinal, and the National Indian Brotherhood of Canada, are examples of this approach.

A second approach, which is more intermittent, arises partly out of the frustration with the apparent slowness of results from the first approach, and partly out of ideological arguments. It consists of confrontation: cross-Canada caravans, demonstrations on Parliament Hill in Ottawa, sit-ins in government offices and national parks, sometimes with a show of arms. This approach has borrowed some strength and leadership from the American Indian Movement (AIM) in the United States.

Both these strategies are familiar to the white world. The first in particular accepts and incorporates the assumptions and features of the political life of that world. To the extent that it does not threaten the basic structures and interests of Canadian society as a whole, it is tolerated and encouraged by the funding of native organizations from government sources. This is one advantage that the Canadian Indians have over the blacks in Rhodesia and South Africa, who are in such a majority that the whites see too great a danger in allowing them any opportunity to form political associations to press for their rights. The Canadian Indians, because of their small numbers, offer no such *initial* threat. But once their demands do begin to threaten the economic and political interests of the dominant white Canadian society, government support is limited or ceases. The posture of the federal government in the face of the native land claims in the Northwest Territories, and of the native people's opposition to the building of a gas pipeline from the Arctic ocean through the Mackenzie valley to southern Canada, and the terms of an agreement negotiated by the Quebec government with the native people of the St James region to enable a huge hydro-electricity scheme to be started in northern Quebec, reveal the limits of white society's tolerance of native people's demands.

In other words, the adoption of a political mode by any group in any situation means the adoption of power as the ultimate instrument of action, and it has to recognize the limitations of relative degrees of power.

The third form taken by Indians to come to grips with their condition is an analysis of that condition in terms of the effect of various institutions on Indian life, and then the formulation of a set of precepts linked back into their cultural traditions. Whereas the leadership in the two other forms of activity has tended to come from amongst younger Indians, this third approach leans heavily on the elders for guidance and interpretation. It involves, therefore, a searching for a solid cultural base, an identity that goes deeper than the sharing of the disadvantages of modern white society, and in this respect it is similar to the re-establishment of identity by colonized African peoples in the 1950s and 1960s, by American blacks in the 1960s, and by American Chicanos today. This building of a collective identity, and its carry-through to the individual, is an important element in the attack which the native people are now making on the problems they face.

Though in their seeking to understand the causes of their present condition they are concerned with institutions and the effects which certain institutions have had on them, and though in turning toward positive solutions they bear these institutions in mind, the emphasis of this approach is on spiritual strength supported by cultural roots. This is the emphasis, for instance, of their attack on one of their biggest problems, alcoholism.

The emphasis is not on political action to change institutional structures, nor on creating their own smooth-running organizations with the help of experts. As a matter of fact, a recent proposal for a fairly sophisticated Indian Education Centre in Alberta, which set out to combine aspects of Indian tradition with western concepts of education and organization, faltered when it failed to obtain the support of Indian elders, who believe that it was not getting to the root of things and was starting 'too high up there.'

What the proponents of this approach have done is to create an analytical tool that suggests the important characteristics of their present condition, and the relationship between these and the factors which have dominated their lives over the last century or so. In Freire's (1972) terms, they have begun to name their world. They have then gone on to suggest the human qualities needed to overcome the present condition, and the way these qualities are symbolized in their culture. The characteristics are: outward hostility; hidden or inner-directed hostility; apathy; and fear. These give rise to grief, but they have the potential to give rise to

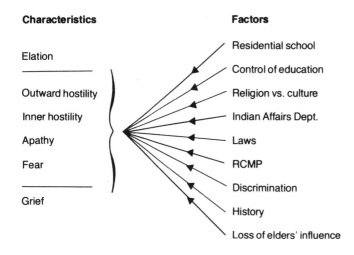

Characteristics

Elation

———————

Outward hostility

Inner hostility

Apathy

Fear

———————

Grief

Factors

Residential school

Control of education

Religion vs. culture

Indian Affairs Dept.

Laws

RCMP

Discrimination

History

Loss of elders' influence

FIGURE 10 Characteristics and factors in Canadian Indian life

elation. The relationship between these characteristics and the factors which have caused them to come about can be shown diagrammatically, as in Figure 10.

For a group of native people to go through an analysis of this sort, taking each factor in turn and seeing how it has contributed on the formation of those four characteristics that are dominant in their lives, is like a purging. For a group of white people to go through the process with native people is to approach an understanding of their grief. It is what one Indian leader, Eddie Bellrose, calls the negative side of the picture.[1]

Starting with the four characteristics – outward hostility, inner (or internecine) hostility, apathy, and fear – there is no need for native people to look hard to see and experience these feelings. They show themselves in high suicide rates, high crime rates, alcoholism, resentment, violence. In other words, they are an ever-present part of the Indian's experience, and they need no lofty conceptualization. Likewise, it is a part of every Indian's experience to have had contact with one or more of the factors which they see as having contributed to the present situation.

Those who had to leave their families to go to residential schools as children recall the loneliness and lostness, and in many cases the indigni-

1 I am indebted to Mr Bellrose, of the Indian Association of Alberta, for this analysis.

ties and insults put upon them by professedly Christian teachers. Some perceive their very move to a distant school as a kind of punishment to their families who showed signs of being obstreperous to the white authorities. And it was in such schools that a foreign religion was laid over their native religion and culture, taking them yet farther from their roots. The fact that the process and content of this education was controlled by others, mainly by various churches, denied them the opportunity to influence their learning and to reinforce that which they absorbed among their own people.

Another cluster of factors which have bitten into the Indian experience has to do with the law and its administration. The Indian Act, a federal law, had the effect of dividing native people into various categories – treaty, non-treaty, and métis (half breed) – and these categories fell under different government jurisdictions – federal and provincial – for many of the basic social services such as health, education, and social assistance. And the administration of the Indian Act to treaty Indians was in the hands of the federal Department of Indian Affairs, whose local agents, all white, were seen at best as paternalistic and usually as authoritarian. With regard to the law in general, extraordinary zeal on the part of the police in applying minor aspects of it, and sometimes downright discrimination in its application as between whites and Indians, has been the experience of many of the latter. Other types of discrimination, such as in employment, service in restaurants, and housing have been a common experience of native people in Canada.

The image of the Indian as savage, pagan, untrustworthy, and generally inferior, has been perpetuated in films and books, and absorbed into western culture to the extent that even Indian children, when playing cowboys and Indians, choose to be cowboys. At a more scholarly level, written history, in its white ethnocentricity, has until recently ignored the role of Indians as statesmen, counsellors, and guides in the early contacts between white and native people.

The course of North American history itself has been seen as the civilizing of pagan and indigent people and the developing of hitherto unappreciated natural resources by good white people. And the Indians themselves have been objects of this process of historical interpretation to the extent that they have lost track of their own sources of wisdom, which are still there among them. In the process of being co-opted, but not integrated, into white society, they have neglected their own elders.

This quick and sketchy description of the main elements in the model set out above gives an indication of the process of self-examination. As a group of Indian people go through the process, some of them may suggest other factors which have affected them and their condition. The process goes further, in that in identifying the factors which have contributed to the present condition, it begins to identify possible ways of rectifying the situation. The clarification of the problem suggests possible courses of action.

This mode of analysis is different from that in model I, in that it starts not with an understanding of broad social and political patterns, but with a look at the human condition shared by the people concerned. Though the analysis comes – implicitly, at any rate – to identify possible courses of action, e.g., efforts to obtain more control of the education agencies or resources, and to bring more responsibility to the working of the Department of Indian Affairs, it takes a different direction. It turns to what are seen to be important elements in the spiritual and cultural life of the Indian people. And the first of these is the elders. As one program co-ordinator at Poundmaker Lodge, a centre for Indian training in Alberta, has said, 'We need to have great respect for the older people. But today we tend to forget them. We want them involved with the younger generation again' (*Edmonton Journal* 1976).

At meetings at which the model is used as a basis of discussion, there are commonly one or more elders present. Their role is to lead the group at the beginning of each day in prayer to the Great Spirit, to begin the ceremony of the pipe, and to give their counsel on current issues by connecting them with past experience and cultural wisdom. So they are restored as a source of inspiration and self-respect. The second part of the model itself starts with the treaties between the Indian people and the Queen through her government of Canada. What the Indian people did *not* give up under the treaties were the mountains, the trees, the grass, and the animals, and therein is their heritage, which they still claim. These are symbolized for the Indians by the pipe, the stem of the pipe, the sweet grass, and the fire. Sweet grass is a prairie grass which, when braided and lit with a match, smoulders in a sweet smoke of incense. These are the symbols. And they are the symbols of, respectively, faith, honesty, kindness, and sharing. So it goes like this: mountains = pipe = faith; trees = stem of pipe = honesty; grass = sweetgrass = kindness; animals = fire = sharing. And these are the values which, according to this analysis, are the real characteristics of the Indian people: faith, honesty, kindness, and sharing. But what is more important is that they are proposed as the values of all people. They are the values which must inform all human relationships. The model leads the Indians through the pain of analysing and seeking the causes of their own condition, toward an examination of the qualities and values which must inform their actions and their relationships with other people.

The first model discussed in this chapter exemplifies the rational, orderly, systematic, and purposeful way of westerners. In the second, purposes and action are only intimated, as in the spaces between the lines in Chinese art. It speaks of what Malinowski (1944,chap. 12) calls the integrative needs, which he suggests exist in us all – the needs which impel us to use religion, myth, and symbolism to cope with those sub- and supra-conscious forces that we fail to bring entirely within our field of knowledge but which move us. If the terms, faith, honesty, kindness, and sharing, have a romantic ring, this is not, I believe, a bad thing. One of the important – and to me acceptable – features of the counter-cultural and consciousness perspectives on social changes is that they bid us recognize that social change, and planning for such change, are not only questions of intellect and rationality but also of spirit, intuition, and subjectivity. To introduce the romantic into perceptions of reality is not naive; it is a part of wisdom. Moreover, it is utilitarian. It is part of the process, referred to in chapter 3, of a people's establishing a group memory with which to confront information received from outside.

The elements of the counter-cultural perspective have the other merit of providing a way for an oppressed minority to re-establish its identity. They provide a suggestion of a bridge between the concept of community as defined in chapter 2 and as it is defined more broadly by McIver and others. The Indian people can take into account their own culture, which is analogous to the older, traditional sense of community, and with the confidence that this engenders they are better equipped to engage in development at the community level in the sense I have defined it.

But the model shares the weakness which Johnson, in discussing Reich's Consciousness III, attributed to the consciousness model of social change (Johnson 1974,chap. 1). Johnson talks of the political naiveté of Reich's position, and 'the optimistic posture that power will ultimately be thwarted by spiritual forces resident within the human soul or heart or psyche' (1974,24). He goes so far as to call Reich's revolution a sham revolution, a call to effect change without any change in the political structures which determine the will and destiny of man. Without going as far as that, it is unlikely that the second model, in itself, will be sufficient to change the real position of the Indian people. They will, in turning toward action, need more focus – groups not only of common interests but common objectives, and planning in pursuit of those objectives.

One might even suggest that for practical social and political purposes the second model might be more effective if it were turned round, so that having articulated and been strengthened by a set of values based on their revived culture, the Indian people would then proceed to analyse the factors in their environment which have helped cause their present condition. And in this their ability to act would be strengthened by their going beyond a statement of the factors set out in the first stage of model II, into a more rigorous process of analysis represented by model I.

The two models outlined in this chapter draw attention to relationships between environmental and cultural factors which constrain or ease social action, whether the action be on the part of individuals or of social groups. They suggest that any group intending to embark on action should be aware of these factors and look at them realistically. The models are analytical in the sense of providing a means of mapping out the present social territory, and in that sense they might be thought of as being static.

But what makes a model static or not is the approach of the person using it to form an understanding of his environment. In certain historical periods of national and international stability there is a tendency for people to feel a static condition, i.e., social stability, as being natural and inherent, and to formulate their perceptions accordingly. In periods of movement and change there is, on the other hand, a tendency to see everything in dynamic terms, and to lose sight of social phenomena which have a restraining effect, such as custom, social structures, and existing resources.

The relationships between the elements of a social system are under constant stress, and there is thus an implied dynamic even within the system as outlined in these two models. One of the main causes of stress is the ways that the behaviour of people in the system affect other people, and in a general way this has entered into the foregoing analysis. But these models do not draw our attention directly to interpersonal relationships – how they come about and how they can influence what goes on in the group. I now want to go on to discuss the dynamics of activities between people within the system, and of these activities in relation to people outside the system: how group behaviour comes about, and how it is influenced by what is outside it. The models in the following chapters address these questions.

6

Groups and group behaviour

What I have been discussing in the previous chapter are ways of taking stock, or making sense, of the society in which the community is situated, with a view to making the efforts of the community as effective as possible. We can call them societal models. They provide means, as I suggested at the end of chapter 4, for what Freire calls the initial decoding stage of the development process, the phase of consciousness raising.

The next phase in the process begins to focus on the community, or group, itself, for it is through the group's efforts that the process will be carried through. In this chapter, therefore, I want to describe two group models which help to sharpen this focus.

A knowledge of group processes is relevant to community development in two ways: first, in relation to learning and second, in relation to action. Much of our learning, about ourselves, about other people, and about the environment, takes place in groups, and having an understanding of group processes helps in that learning.

The first of the two group models draws attention to the transition from consideration of the broad environment to the activities of the group in that environment. It helps, in other words, to place the group in its societal context.

HOMANS' MODEL

Homans' definition of a group is congruent with the idea proposed in chapter 2 that in the initial stages of the community development process we have not a community of people with a common and agreed objective marhsalled in their purposes and energies toward the attainment of that objective, but a collection of people who simply interact with one another, or 'participate together in social events.' (Homans 1950,84). The group, according to Homans, is defined by the interactions of its members, irrespective of the particular activities in which they interact. So here is the original point of departure, the primitive human group, where the process of community development starts.

In the first place, the identity of the group becomes established by seeing which persons and groups one chooses to consider outsiders to the group in question, and this act of identification can take place both from within the collection of people, subjectively, and from outside, objectively. In other words, a groupness can be something which either grows spontaneously or purposefully from within, as people begin to interact together more than they react, as individuals, with other people, or is thrust upon them by the perceptions and judgments of other people. In some cases, particularly ethnic minorities, or counter-cultural groups, the groupness is attributed first from the outside, against the desires of the members, whose wish is not to be distinguished and isolated, but then, as the distinction feeds on itself in the minds of the 'others,' i.e., the majority, a defensive process of inner identification takes place, and there comes into being what Homans calls a social system (1950,87) in 'the activities, interactions, and sentiments of the group members, together with the mutual relations of these elements with one another during the time the group is active.' And from these activities, interactions, and sentiments arise a set of group norms.

So the development of the initial group into a social system comes about with the emergence of a pattern not simply of interaction and participation, but also of sentiment. Until all these factors are present, i.e., activities, interactions, and sentiments, there can be no real group, and there is no beginning from which a process of community development can advance. This is brought out clearly in the predicament of some of the native people in northern Canada. There is an area near Whitehorse in the Yukon, where a number of native people are strung out in small family collections along the highway and rivers. The growing economic activity in the area raises in these people an uneasiness about their ways and values of life. At one level they have formed the Yukon Native Brotherhood, but at the ground level the problem of articulating a concern and getting together to do something about it still exists. And it seems that the position they are in during the initial period – in the early 1970s – is that there is not sufficient communication – i.e., activities and interactions – between them, and they have not been able to generate enough commonly expressed sentiments and spiritual identity, to move them forward as a group.[1] In chapter 2, I discussed the same problem in relation to the concept of community among Blacks in Africa and the United States, and Indians in Canada. The formulation of a group spirit follows from the formulation of sentiments and feelings between the people, and this cannot normally happen without communication between people, and authorities who feel the threat of potential communities in their jurisdiction will often attempt to cut off communication between the members of such potential communities. Communication, then, is a primary point to be borne in mind by a worker who is invited by a group of people, whether they be inner-city people or Native people being confronted with a new way of life, to come and help them sort themselves out.

The establishment of the identity of a group by seeing which persons and groups one chooses to consider outsiders is also a process of establishing the boundaries of the group. And the concept of group, community, and system boundaries is a useful one in the study of these units of human activity.

To link the group with its environment, Homans discusses two elements: the environment itself and the external system of the group.

THE ENVIRONMENT

The environment is that which lies outside the boundaries of the group. Homans suggests that in its relationship with its environment a human group lies somewhere on a scale between the human body and a thermodynamic system such as a cup of hot coffee. The human body has a formidable capacity to maintain a steady state in the face of changes in the environment, while the capacity of a cup of hot coffee to do so is very limited, and it has virtually no capacity to act on its environment. The human group cannot disregard the demands of the environment, but it is not completely passive; it shares a property with the animal body, which is to struggle toward the free life. It shares, likewise, a property which humanistic psychologists attribute to each individual person, as we saw in chapter 4 in discussing learning theories and models of the nature of man, in a capacity not just to react passively to stimuli from outside, but to symbolize, synthesize, explore, and affect the environment (Hampton-Turner 1970,chap. 111.) Applying this proposition to groups, Homans shows how the group of workers in the bank wire room of the Western

---

1 I am indebted for this example to my colleague, Glen Eyford, Director, Division of Community Development, at the University of Alberta.

Electric Hawthorne plant, where Mayo, Roethlisberger, and others did their pioneer studies on human aspects of management, had an impact on their environment by restricting output. The environment of the bank wiring group was the Western Electric Works at Hawthorne.

I have had occasion to work with a housing co-operative in Alberta (i.e., a co-operative that is concerned not only with co-operating in the building of houses but also with the building and maintaining of a community spirit through sharing). The group went through a period of crisis in the planning stage, which was related largely to forces in the environment which impinged on the ideas of the co-operative, and they revolved around day-care and laundry facilities. The day-care issue arose out of the delays and problems in financing, which had to do with the policy and requirements of the city government and its funding agencies with regard to day-care facilities. The laundry issue arose out of the requirement of the Central Mortgage and Housing Corporation – the main source of funds for the co-operative – that instead of a common laundry facility each housing unit must have its own washing machine and drier. The people in the co-operative had to negotiate with the agencies concerned, to implement their ideas.

Homans suggests three aspects of the environment of a group – physical, technical, and social. The *physical* aspect relates to where the group is, the shape of its surroundings, the natural conditions such as climate. The *technical* aspect of the environment comprises the tools, artifacts, and – these days – the whole paraphernalia of electronic hardware which intrudes almost everywhere. The *social* aspect consists of the influences from outside the group, its relationships with other groups and other social institutions such as local government bodies, in other words, the sum of sentiments, activities, and interactions in other groups. These relations may be informal, as between different street corner gangs, or formal, as between tenants' associations and municipal governments. They are also bound to include the wider influences of the culture in which the group exists, such as relationships between a black minority group and a majority white population, and the values and norms that exist in the society in which the group exists. The environment of the native groups in the Yukon, regarded under these headings, will include: the *physical* environment – the great distances, the short days and long nights of winter, the cold and snow as they affect communication; the *technical* environment – the highway system and the vehicles, including the snowmobile, helicopter, and aeroplane; radio, and the establishment of the Anik satellite as a television link; the *social* environment – the tribal culture, the Native

Brotherhood, the relations with white merchants, mining company and government officials. All these are clearly interrelated and they affect one another: the transport facilities and the physical isolation; radio and television and the other tribal customs; the Native Brotherhood and the government officials.

Homans defines the external system as the state of the sentiment, activity, and inter-action within the group which constitutes a solution – not necessarily the only solution – of the problem of how the group is to survive in its environment. What is done in the group, and what feelings exist in the group, which enables it to meet the demands made upon it by the environment, and which legitimizes the existence of the group? In the external system sentiment is represented by the motives the persons have for being in the group – motives of economic security, social respect as a worker, fulfilment as a family-supporter, prestige in the society. The activities are what people in the group do to fulfil their formal role in the group, and the interactions are the ways in which they have contact with one another in the performance of their roles. If a group has no such system of sentiments, activities, and interactions, and the sort of antennae which enable it to adjust these in such a way as to meet the requirements of the environment, then it stands the grave risk of ceasing to exist. This is the fate of extreme radical (right or left) or revolutionary groups which cannot bring themselves to acknowledge the realities of their environment, and persist in declaring themselves and behaving in a way that makes no concessions to the state of the political environment in which they exist. And insofar as such groups do continue to exist, they really exist in some other capacity than that in which they *ostensibly* exist; they cease to be aimed at changing things but become aimed at meeting some other need (generally not admitted) of the members of the group.

This raises the question of the objectives of groups. In chapter 2, in discussing the concept of community, I observed that it is not unknown for organizations, particularly voluntary organizations, to become moribund, because the objectives with which they were formed have been achieved, or frustrated, or ignored. Homans, in his main study, does not talk directly about the objectives of groups, i.e., *why* the members of the group interact, to what purpose the sentiments, activities, and interactions are there. He refers to the motives of the workers in the bank wiring room at the Hawthorne plant, but in their capacity as sentiments within the group (i.e., on the part of *individual members*) which help the group meet the requirements of the environment. But the implication of his proposition about the external system of the group, i.e., that which enables it to survive in the environment, is that the *group's* objectives are related to this survival. A group has as part of its objective something that has to do with its position in the environment: to change it by getting better housing, or a community hall, or better wages, and so on, or simply to be tolerated by it. This latter position would be that of some nudist cults, communes, and religious orders. These may, and sometimes do, have in mind an ultimate goal of making the world a better place for all by their example, but to do this they must have a more immediate objective of survival in order to be perceived as an example, and this makes a certain minimum demand on their external system.

THE INTERNAL SYSTEM

Homans then proposes a third element of the group's being: its internal system. Social life, says Homans, is never wholly utilitarian (i.e., existing for some purpose outside the group): it elaborates itself, complicates itself, beyond the demands of the original situation, i.e., of the motives the group members had when they originally joined the group (1950,109). Another set of activities, interactions, and sentiments comes into being, which are not directly conditioned by the environment. Something spontaneous happens within the group, which relates to the needs of group members in relation to one another. The sentiments which thus arise are feelings – likings and dislikings – which group members have about one another; the activities are the expressions and the acting out of these feelings; the interactions are the fun, play, and contests that take place between members as a result of liking and disliking. And these elements of the internal system form another order of objectives of the group, objectives which are internal to the group and which meet the needs of the individual members of the group. Groups are, therefore, something more than units of people with an external goal – utilitarian, as Homans puts it. They form an environment which enables individuals to meet very personal needs.

There are mutual relationships between the three elements of the internal system (sentiments, activities, and interactions) as well as between them and the elements of the external system. For instance, Homans suggests, on the basis of his analysis of the bank wiring room group, that 'if the interactions between the members of a group are frequent in the external system, sentiments of liking will grow up between them, and these sentiments will lead in turn to further interactions, over and above the interactions of the external system' (1950,112). In other words, between those members of a group who come into frequent contact in their work on the group's task, there will tend to develop good feelings, and an increase of contacts over and above what the job requires. Furthermore, the less members of the group interact with people *outside* the group, and the more they feel negative toward them, the more they will tend to interact with and have good feelings for people inside the group. This is the common experience of being brought closer together by an outside enemy.

By drawing our attention to the two systems of relationships in a group: the external system and the internal system, Homans introduces us to a feature of group life which is important for community development. Community development has a practical purpose, i.e. a change in the condition of the people involved in the process, and as far as possible of the environment of which they are a part, so there is the danger of concentrating too much attention on the achievement of such change, i.e., the completion of the task of the community. In doing this we are in danger of looking at the external system and ignoring the internal system – the interplay of sentiments, activities, and interactions of people in the group which have little to do with the needs of the group in relation to the environment, but which bear on the effectiveness of the group in the meeting of these needs. This is an important point; we have to keep in mind, as members of a community, the emotional state of the membership and how it shows itself in various behaviours, because a poor emotional state can frustrate the efforts of the group to reach its objective. In my army days, without having read anything of social psychology, we used the term 'morale' and 'good man-management.' If the concepts were somewhat crude in that they had more to do with strong direction from a formal leader than with inner group strength, they nonetheless reflected a consciousness of the problems of intra-group relations. But even today, after over two decades of further research into and the popularization of group dynamics, there are plenty of community and occupational group leaders whose appreciation of the importance of the internal system of sentiments, activities, and interactions is minimal, and who see the group's existence only in terms of its overt objectives.

Taking Homans' point that several different sets of words are available for the expression of a single idea (1950,137), we can suggest that the operations of the external system and internal system are comparable to the task function and the social-emotional or maintenance function, which other writers have identified in groups. It is these two functions to which the next model draws attention.

While there is a link, through the Homans' model, between considerations of the environment (chapter 5) and of group activities in the environment, there is another link between considerations of learning models and their underlying assumptions about the nature of man and social behaviour on the one hand (chapter 4), and group dynamics on the other.

One immediate connection lies in the seminal work done by Kurt Lewin in this field. We saw in chapter 4 how Lewin's notion of perception as being affected by one's life space was an important part of the formulation of the cognitive learning model. Beyond that, Lewin's interest in learning and motivation as part of the whole question of personality development led him to take a primary role in the early studies of group dynamics and in the formation of the National Training Laboratory (later known as the NTL Institute for Applied Behavioral Science) which became a focal point for theoretical and practical work related to group processes (Luft 1970,chap. 1). It was through the NTL Institute and other similar operations such as the Research Centre for Group Dynamics at the University of Michigan that this field of study was applied to organizations – in McGregor's terms, the human side of enterprise (1960). And what has been referred to as the human relations movement, or the human relations approach to management, had, and has, as its leaders many who would identify themselves with the cognitive learning model.

It is, I believe, not an accident that it was in the United States that this movement had its early impetus. The United States displays the most advanced condition of the industrial, free-enterprise economy, based on individualist values, capitalism, and competition, and it is there that signs of tension between individual well-being and personal values on the one hand, and organizational effectiveness and mass technology on the other, began to be noticed and cause concern. It was out of that concern that the human relations movement emerged, with its interest in personal fulfilment on the job – a reaction against the classical theory of management and its emphasis on centralized authority, control, close supervision, and depersonalization. And one of the central tools in the human relations approach to organizational life was the use of experiential group situations for the study and practice of interpersonal communication, participation, and leadership (Etzioni 1964,chap. 5). Likewise, I believe it is not accidental that the human relations approach to management, originating as it did in the United States, does not pretend to disturb the basic structures of a free-enterprise capitalist economy, and I shall allude to this again later in discussing organization development.

There are two kinds of people whom one commonly finds engaged in community work. One is the active, energetic, and purposeful sort of person exemplified by the chairman of a local community league – commonly a businessman or member of a profession. Such people are, it seems, devoted to the causes of the community, and when issues arise they like to hustle them through to a successful conclusion. The other sort of person shows the characteristics of the sensing-feeling person described by Mogar and referred to in chapter 4 as being interested in people and social service. People of this sort – who often find their way into social service work in government and quasi-government agencies – commonly have a feeling for interpersonal relationships and are more concerned with the fostering of such relationships than hustling through toward clearcut and utilitarian objectives. In one group of students in which I have worked the total group split, by a process of discussion, into two groups which showed these opposite characteristics, and they called themselves the Human Theory Project Group and the Pheelies, respectively.

The group process model which I now propose to describe is useful for both these types of people. It helps each to appreciate the stance of the other, and when used for training purposes it provides an opportunity to reflect on their own style of behaviour and its effect on the total group behaviour. This model concentrates on the internal working of groups. I shall not attempt to cover the whole field of group theory and practice, but to outline one of the fundamental features that is relevant to the two styles and personalities which I have referred to above. Though I have said above that group dynamics as applied to organizational life was given its impetus in the United States, and though this model was elaborated by American social scientists, it originated in the work of an Englishman.

BION MODEL

W.R. Bion was a psychotherapist working at the Tavistock Institute in London. Although the groups from which he drew his analysis were therapeutic groups, in contrast to the occupational and community groups studies by Homans, the dynamics proposed by Bion from his observations are relevant for the work of people like community workers who are concerned with group organization and effectiveness. First of all, in relation to the group seen as a whole, Bion suggests a number of qualities which go to make up 'good group spirit.' The qualities which Bion (1961,25-6) suggests a good group must have are (a) a common purpose; (b) common recognition by members of the group of the boundaries of the group; (c) a capacity to absorb new members and lose existing ones without fear for the group's character; (d) freedom from exclusive internal sub-groups; (e) freedom for each member to contribute, within the generally accepted conditions devised and imposed by the group. Members valued for their contribution; (f) the group must have the capacity to face and cope with dissent; (g) a minimum size of three, to allow for interpersonal relationships.

Within the group as a whole, Bion postulated the existence of a 'work group' and a 'basic-assumption group.' The work group is in operation when the members of the group are co-operating to achieve the purposes of the group – when, in other words, the objectives and the task of the group are dominant and are not being, in Bion's words, 'swamped by the emotional states' of the members. These emotional states, Bion suggests, are of three kinds: flight-fight, dependency, and pairing. And these three kinds of emotional state create the basic assumption or modalities of the group, which he labels as basic-assumption flight-fight, basic-assumption dependency, and basic-assumption pairing.[2]

The flight-fight modality is one which Bion suggests is a way of preserving the group, that is, group self-preservation. *Flight* is a condition in which the group runs away from the emotional needs of one or more members of the group – in the case of Bion's groups, from the neuroses of an individual or individuals in the group. This can happen by bringing up matters from outside the group's immediate experience, talking about other events, physically moving into another activity – 'anyone for tennis?' *Fight* is a condition in which, instead of running away from such an individual emotional need, the tendency is to fight it, in subtle or in open ways – to deflate it or to bash it down. This takes the form of sarcasm, a put-down, or even open hostility. The *pairing* modality arises from a condition in which two individual members of a group enter into a close relationship with each other to cope with problems or to achieve some personal satisfaction, and in

2 Incidentally, in connection with my discussion in the introduction of how concepts are rational representations of experience, Bion's account of how he conceptualized the actual goings-on in his therapeutic groups is a good example of the way concepts are refined as the result of experience. Bion (1961,61) says, 'the group changed in ways that left me stranded and not able to apply my theories in any way that convinced me.' So he was continually adjusting his theories.

which the other members of the group are prepared to let this happen, as if it met some wider and implicit need of these other members. The *dependency* modality characterizes a phase off the group's life where members are seeking support from, i.e., are dependent on, a person or institution which they see as being stronger than them, and this is generally the formal leader of the group – possibly the community development worker.

To refer to phases in the group's life is to point to an important feature of Bion's argument, which is that a group can move into and out of any of these three modalities in the course of its existence, for short or long periods. It can also move backward and forward from one of these modalities to the 'work group' modality, so the progress of a group toward its declared objective can be uneven, and thus frustrating to a task-oriented member or leader.

Bion goes on to suggest that individuals have what he calls valences, or readinesses, to enter into one of these three modalities. He suggests that to have no such valence is to cease to be human (1961,116). A valence is what Bion calls a proto-mental phenomenon, an inner and pre-conscious emotional state that underlies the basic assumption, and that rises to the surface in observable behaviour. So as the group develops its members' pre-conscious states become visible in these types of behaviour, and the whole group goes into one of the 'basic assumption' groups.

Individual valences, therefore, become an important element in the functioning of any group, and this bears on the suggestion in chapter 2 that it is important for members of a group to acquire a knowledge of themselves, an important part of themselves being their individual valences. Do I tend toward a mode of fight or flight, or dependency, or pairing, or toward a work role? Am I task-oriented or do I tend to let my emotional needs get in the way? If a significant number of other members of the group tend towards one of these modes, what effects can this have in the functioning of the group in relation to its 'external' task?

These points can be illustrated, and investigated by the reader, through an instrument fashioned to enable individuals to see what valence they tend toward. It consists of a sheet of fifty statements, each ending with two alternative descriptions of behaviour, one of which is selected by each person as being nearer to representing the way he would act in the situation. The instrument is called a test of reactions to group situation.[3] Here are two examples.

3 See appendix B; reproduced by permission of Dr Herbert Thelen, University of Chicago, who formulated it.

When I wanted to work with Frank, I ...
A felt we could do well together
B asked if it would be all right with him

The scoring key to the test suggests that response A indicates a pairing valence, while B indicates a dependency valence.

When the leader changed the subject, I ...
A suggested that they stick to the original topic
B felt glad that the leader was finally taking over

The key suggests that response A indicates a work valence and B a dependency valence.

A final tally of one's score gives an indication of one's tendency toward one or more valences. The test directions ask that the selections be made quickly, without reflection and possible rationalization, presumably in order to try to adhere to Bion's proposition that valences are proto-mental or pre-conscious. Such a test is, of course, a fairly gross one, since the mere act of articulating one of the two alternative responses brings the process forward into one's consciousness, and it may involve the justification of one's self-concept and thus, in terms of subsequent behaviour, an element of self-fulfilling prophecy. This, however, seems to be a danger in any mode of self-revelation or of feedback about oneself by someone else, and to entirely deny its validity is to question the validity of most ways of seeking self-knowledge.

Bion's modalities were used by Bennis and Shepard in the United States to develop further the body of theoretical concepts about group behavior (Bennis and Shepard 1956, 415-38). Using the laboratory method applied in T-groups, they analysed the process a group went through, in terms of power relations between the group members and the group leader, or trainer, and between group members themselves, and the personal relations between members and leader. Power relations are acted out within the dimension of dependence and it is within this dimension that the greater part of the early life of the group takes place as applied to T-groups, where the trainer abrogates the traditional role of leader by not directing and ordering the affairs of the group. The initial phase of this early period of dependence shows up the group's feeling of *dependence in various forms of flight*: introducing matters that occurred outside the group, 'at home'; allowing assertive group members to bring out their previous experience as badges of identity; dwelling on the outside world and the 'there-and-then.' There is a studious ignoring or denigration of the authority of the trainer. Then comes a phase of *counter-dependence, or fight*: discussion about getting organization into the group; oblique fighting between members and distrust of the trainer; the formation of two cliques – the aggressive counter-dependents and the non-aggressive dependents; and finally, in this phase revolving around the issue of dependence, there is a degree of *resolution*, by pairing or by concentration on a group task, by developing an internal system of authority, and possibly by the engineering of the deposition of the trainer as leader. All this revolves around the issue of *dependence*, or *power* relationships.

Bennis and Shepard suggest that some groups do not get beyond this stage, in other words, that they remain at a stage where the chief underlying issue is one of power relations within the group. There can even be a reversion from a later phase to an earlier one – from 'resolution,' to 'fight.' But if the process does go further it develops into one which revolves around the issue of *interdependence*, or personal, as distinct from power, relations. From the phase of resolution and strong task orientation there develops a phase of what they call 'enchantment.' There is a sense of solidarity and camaraderie between group members, rejection of the trainer and a sharing of dominance among the members, expression of understanding of how the group has developed. Bennis and Shepard characterize the emotional tone of the group in this phase as 'pairing-flight.' There then develops a phase of 'disenchantment,' characterized in its emotional tone as 'fight-flight,' where distrust and suspicion arise between members, and a re-questioning of what the group is all about. Some members go absent; those having a high need for affection and intimacy feel let down and are depressed, and sub-groups form to cope with anxiety. And finally, there comes a phase of what the authors call 'consensual validation,' with pairing and acceptance. The personal ties diminish, there is a more realistic acceptance of the group and of the total experience which it has undergone, and a turning toward the external realities. The group, in other words, turns from an exclusive preoccupation with its internal workings, or basic assumptions, to the job at hand in the environment in which the group exists.

It is perhaps in this sense that Bennis and Slater (1969,86) suggest that one of the values and capacities learned in a T-group experience is how to cope with movement in and out of temporary systems. The final phase of understanding and acceptance shows the group members as coming to terms with the whole experiernce and its meaning for them as people who also live in other groups, even in other environments, to which they must return now that this group, this 'temporary system,' has come to an end. And thus, by undergoing such an experience a few times, a kind of inner capacity is acquired to deal with the mobility, change, and broken intimacies of the kind of life that more and more people are subjected to these days.

There is much that can be transferred from the experience of т-groups to an understanding of working groups. In fact, the human relations movement, of which the т-group has been a central instrument, has deliberately seen such groups as *training* groups, and not as *therapeutic* groups of the Bion sort – 'training' in the sense of providing a learning experience that will help individuals understand and cope with other group situations in which they work or live. The early emphasis was on a study of group processes. This aspect remains important, and even predominant, in what the NTL Institute calls its Basic Human Relations Laboratories.

This brief discussion of the Bion model of group processes as developed by Bennis and Shepard, has dealt with what Homans calls the internal system of the group. Without requiring that those working in community development should have all the nuances of this theoretical analysis at their fingertips while being engaged with groups, an awareness of the dynamics of *group* behaviour (because an important part of Bion's theory is that the group assumes a behaviour and a personality apart from those of the members) will help such workers have more realistic expectations of working groups. It also introduces a distinction which has become an important element in subsequent group theory and practice, and that is the distinction between task functions and socio-emotional or maintenance functions. These relate to the two sorts of people sketched out earlier in this chapter. At some points in time the need for leadership in the group lies in working on and improving the emotional state of the group, and some individuals are good at that and they exercise leadership insofar as they perform in that way. At other times, the need is to get on with the task, and here others may perform better as leaders.

That is one way in which this model can be adapted so as to serve a practical purpose in the process of learning in community development, i.e., in learning about oneself and one's behavioural tendencies in groups. Another way is the technique formulated by Bales for observing and analysing what is going on in a group, (i.e., participant observation) (Sprott 1958,130-3). This system is based on the concept of task-oriented functions and social-emotional functions, and Bales breaks these down into twelve types of behaviour which are observable and can be related to the two functions.

In the group process the behaviours which tend to be task-oriented are: giving or asking for suggestions or directions in a way which implies autonomy for the others in the group; giving or asking for an opinion, evaluation, analysis, or expression of feeling; providing or asking for orientation, information, confirmation, or recapitulation.

The behaviours which have a positive value with regard to the social-emotional state of the group are: showing solidarity by raising others' status, giving help, rewarding; releasing tension with jokes and laughter, and showing appreciation; agreeing by showing passive acceptance, understanding, and concurrence.

And the behaviours which have a negative value with regard to the socio-emotional state of the group are: showing disagreement by passive rejection, formality, and withholding help; showing tension by asking for help and withdrawing; showing antagonism by deflating others' status, or defending or asserting oneself.

By being aware of these behaviours in oneself one can practice at being a more effective group member; by being able to observe and evaluate these behaviours in others one can often, as an invited observer, give useful feedback to a working group about some of the things that are going on in the group which help or hinder it in its purposes. This is sometimes the role that a community development worker is invited to perform for a community group. For instance, the cases of the co-operative described earlier were related not only to substantial issues such as daycare and laundry facilities but also to personality and status among members, and the behaviours shown in relation to these factors. Some of these difficulties have been eased by inviting to meetings of the group an observer whose role is to provide feedback to the members on the dynamics of their behaviour.

In one important sense the learning experiences comprising mainly T-groups, which have been suggested as useful training for community group leaders, are artificial. What they do is to remove the participants to a reasonably isolated place, cut off from the distractions of working life, to form a cultural island. On this island they can isolate and concentrate on those aspects of group and organization life which are commonly not dealt with 'at home,' because most working situations create a pressure on people to get on with the task of the organization. At home a good deal of the emotional tension that builds up is not confronted, and gets in the way of achieving that task. Informal groups spring up which can effectively sabotage the task of the formal organization. And this can happen in communities. Toward the end of a human relations laboratory, there-

fore, the design of the laboratory will include an opportunity for participants to relate their learning in the laboratory to their back-home situation.

Since the efficacy of this final stage of such experience has been shown
in practice to be doubtful, because each participant is about to return to an
organizational setting in which other people have not had these experiences and are still engaged in the work-a-day problems surrounding
them, a later development was the institution of 'family laboratories,' that
is, group experiences that have as their participants members of one organization. Such experiences are often included as part of an organization
development process, which I discuss in the following chapter. This is an
attempt, in other words, to place the internal dynamics of a working
group in their immediate working setting.

FROM GROUP DYNAMICS TO ORGANIZATIONAL CHANGE

So both these writers draw attention to a point which figures dominantly
in the literature of group dynamics: the distinction between task function
on the one hand and social-emotional functions on the other hand (Bales
1950; Bennis and Sheats 1961). It is a point which bears on the exercise of
control and leadership in groups (Haiman 1951,88-102; Thelen 1954,
chaps. 10 and 11). Homans goes on to develop this line of thinking in a
way which is important for community development. He relates the internal dynamics and workings of the group to its environment, through
his concept of the external system. In other words, no group, and no community, is isolated from an environment which impinges on it and makes
certain demands on it.

We have seen how group dynamics, which takes so much from Bion
and the Tavistock Institute on the one hand, and the Lewin/NTL/Michigan
stream on the other, became the basis of the human relations approach to
management and organizational change. This approach emphasized individual learning and changes of behaviour as a factor in organizational
change. Make individuals such as workers, supervisors, and managers
better at self-understanding and interpersonal communication, by send-
ing them off to group process laboratories, and you will make the organizations to which they belong more effective.

It was because of a growing experience that individual change had its
limitations as a means of wider organizational and social change that
there has been a move toward a study of social and organizational units.
From its early years the NTL Institute has played a role in relation to com-

munity development, particularly through the work of Curtis and Dorothy Mial (1961), and it continues to include in its program at least one community development workshop each year. And the group dynamics movement in general has always been strongly represented in community development training and practice by such people as Thelen, Moe, and Lippitt. In such training some of the techniques and skills developed in the field of group dynamics, such as T-groups and interpersonal communication exercises, are important components. But in recent years the dominant thrust of the NTL Institute, and probably the majority of practitioners in the field, has been into organizational development. This development has been led by Bennis (1969) and Beckhard (1969). Organization development proceeds on the basis that organizational change depends not only on individual change and the improvement of interpersonal relations, but also on structural change within the organization, i.e., changes in the relationships between roles, particularly around decision-making, and between people and the technologies with which they work.

These sorts of relationships have been taken up in the Tavistock tradition and developed through the work of Trist, Emery, and Rice in the study of socio-technical systems, in other words, the ways that people operate in the context of work groups which, in turn, operate with certain techniques toward certain organizational and work goals (Emery and Trist 1969; Rice 1957). What the socio-technical system approach adds to all this is the consideration of the specific environment of the organization. It is in this respect that there has been, in later studies, whether explicitly or not, an element of Homans' concept that there is an unavoidable relationship between what happens in the internal system of the group and what happens in the external system as affected by the environment.

In the next chapter I shall follow this line of thought through a discussion of the relevance to community development of organization development and socio-technical systems. The discussion will point toward the usefulness of these concepts in the decision-making phase of community development.

7

Organization development and socio-technical systems

For workers in community development the principles of organization development are useful in two ways: first, they provide a bridge between theories of group process discussed in the previous chapter and of larger systems which we have discussed in chapter 3; second, they reveal a particular approach to a study of the functioning of organizations and of techniques or strategies of change in organizations, so they have something to say to the actual process of problem-solving and planning in groups – which will be the subject of the next chapter.

Let me take up the discussion from a point toward the end of the chapter 6, where I indicated how the study of group processes has moved from an emphasis on individual change to change in the organization to which the individual belonged. I referred to the work that had developed from the base of Bion's analysis at the Tavistock Institute in London, into the field of socio-technical systems, and the work that had developed in the United States from the base of group dynamics, T-group theory, and the human relations approach to organizational change. Important common elements in both developments are that both are concerned with human systems, that is, a set of relationships between *people*, and that such systems are seen as open systems, that is, systems in which there is an input and an output of energies and resources which cause changes in the components of the system. They therefore concern themselves with growth and change rather than stability. Vaill (1967) suggests that there is considerable empirical evidence that human systems undergo many equilibrium-disturbing experiences and that as a result they change rather than returning to old patterns. This is a different concept from that inherent in the structural-functional approach of, for example, Malinowski, which relates behaviour to a presumably stable system of needs and mechanisms, and where the basic need is seen as the maintenance of the equilibrium of the system (Selznick 1969,267-8).

The concept of the open system also emphasizes the importance of the environment, from which come the inputs which influence change in the system and to which go outputs which may in turn help change the environment. In other words, the system is not merely passive, changing in response to environmental influences, but can influence change in the environment. The definition of an organization by Lawrence and Lorch as 'an active system which tends to reach out and order its otherwise overly complex surroundings so as to cope with them effectively' conveys this sense of activeness rather than passiveness (Lawrence and Lorch 1969,230).

These two approaches have two important features. They emphasize the open systems element in institutional change, and they go beyond the human relations approach by drawing attention to the technological aspects of organizational life. Whereas the human relations approach stresses the social and psychological situation of men at work, the socio-technical systems approach shows the importance of the actual job – its technology and its physical and mechanical requirements (Emery and Trist 1969,284). The important point for those working in community development is that it is necessary, in working on change in systems, and in groups within systems (subsystems), to take into account not only the human elements but the technology and the structure within the system, and the environment of the system. And technology, in the sense used by these writers, means not just the hardware used in the organization, but the relationships between the hardware and the people working with it, as well as the way the hardware influences the relationships and interactions between people, as on an assembly line operation. It is in this respect, for example, that one uses the term 'educational technology' as being the way that instructional media affect the process of human learning, and the relationships between the teacher and the learner and between learners in the classroom.

The term 'technology,' used in this context, therefore becomes a way, or a set of techniques, of doing things – of bringing together the co-operative activity of a group of people in conjunction with tools and machines, in order to achieve some goal (Vaill 1967,53). One can therefore include in the category of socio-technical systems a community group working with video equipment and cable TV to set up a community television service, or a co-operative housing association working with drawing boards, flow charts, architectural and land-use designs, by-laws, buildings, etc., to achieve a planned and co-operative housing scheme.

I shall deal first with the socio-technical systems model because it carries further, by a process of closer analysis, the examination of the relationship of the environment to a community's internal life, which the Homans model introduced. The environment with which the socio-technical systems model is concerned is that which immediately surrounds and relates to the community's goals, i.e., the task environment. In other words, we are narrowing in on goals and task. The model enables us to look carefully at goals and the action sub-system established to achieve those goals.

I will then return to the transition from emphasis on individual change to organizational change which I alluded to at the end of the last chapter. That will lead into the decision-making phase of the community development process.

SOCIO-TECHNICAL SYSTEMS

In the socio-technical systems model we begin with two basic elements of the open system: its goals and its environment, which is here called the task environment, i.e., the environment which is relevant to the task and goals for which the system exists. In socio-technical systems terminology this task is of primary importance; in fact, the term 'primary task' is what it all hinges upon, for the primary task is the purpose for which the system exists and which it is created to achieve (Miller 1954,243). It corresponds to the community's objective in chapter 2. The next element is the system boundaries, that is, the way in which the system is distinguished from its environment and from other systems. If the system is seen as a cluster of relationships, then areas of less intense relationships become potential boundaries between systems and subsystems. Within these boundaries the system consists of a set of inputs, outputs, and throughputs, the latter making up the transformation element of the system. In most systems there are both intended and unintended outputs, and since outputs are the means by which the system seeks to attain its goals, the production of unintended outputs diverts from these goals, and causes what is called system variance. It is this system variance which ultimately one seeks to discover and remove in order to bring about beneficial change in the operation of the system. It sets the terms of reference for a process of organizational change. The system is illustrated diagrammatically in Figure 11, and I will take the housing co-operative, referred to earlier, to illustrate my discussion of the system.

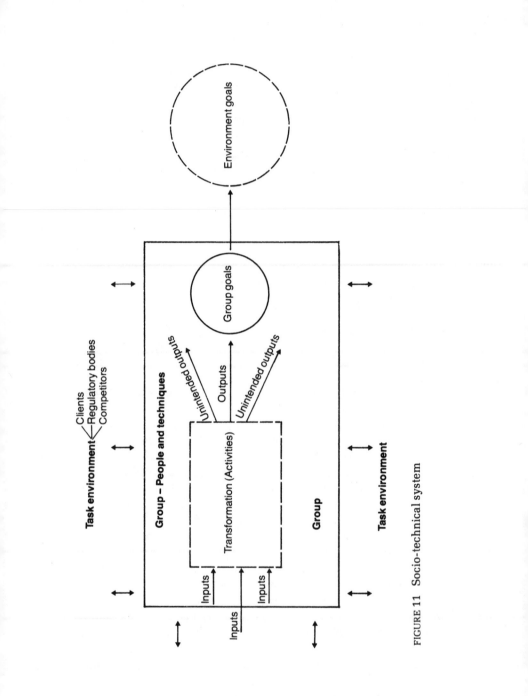

FIGURE 11 Socio-technical system

PRIMARY TASK

One can assume that the primary task of the co-operative is to erect and maintain a group of housing units appropriate to the wants and financial resources of the members of the co-operative. If it is a true co-operative an important part of this task is to arrive at decisions about management, locality, and design by a democratic process in which all members participate directly, and to continue the management of the venture by the same process. This raises an important point about this kind of institution, and about community development in general, which distinguishes them from more task-oriented institutions such as army units and profit-earning business enterprises. In co-operative and other community development ventures the primary task, or objective, has to do as much with the *process* of group action as with its *content*. In fact, community development has attracted the criticism that some of its proponents are so interested in the process that they lose the sense of practicality that directs attention to the need for content and end product. I have referred to one such criticism by Erasmus, in chapter 2 (Erasmus 1968).

For a housing co-operative the process by which the end product is achieved, i.e., the houses and their lay-out, is an essential element of their objectives, and the members are as concerned about obtaining a certain degree of involvement and community decision-making as they are about the ultimate shape of the housing development and the design of the unit. It is, in fact, such involvement which will determine these shapes and designs. But it goes beyond this; it is a way of living as a community, expressing and experiencing a certain philosophy and system of values, which is central to the co-operative's objectives. This can be contrasted to the assumptions and expectations in a housing scheme produced by a private developer or a public housing agency for customers who will rent or buy the houses. The housing co-operative differs from the operations of the private developer in not being concerned to make a profit – which can be said to be the primary task of the developer – and from the operations of both the private developer and the public housing agency in being interested in the occupants not just as individual tenants or purchasers but as fellow members in a joint community effort.

The distinction is, therefore, not simply one of degrees of participation in decision-making. Even in organizations based on the profit motive, and even in army units, there has in recent years been an increasing interest in encouraging worker-involvement and in creating better interpersonal relationships. In a housing co-operative of the sort we are considering the internal 'community-ness' is crucial and explicit.

TASK ENVIRONMENT

So what is the task environment of the co-operative? In particular, what other institutions and systems in the environment impinge on the co-operative and affect its ability to realize its goals? There is a narrower focus to this question than to the examination of the environment discussed in chapter 5. There we were concerned with the problem of generally surveying the total environment in which the group existed, at the stage before it had formulated its objectives, in other words, an orientation of the group to its environment. The objectives subsequently take shape in the light of such an orientation. We are now looking at the stage where objectives are formed and the community as a system is applying itself to the attainment of these objectives. We can narrow our survey down to those elements in the environment which affect that process. In doing so we may discover that it is necessary to go back to the wider survey of the type discussed in chapter 5 and re-examine some of our conclusions.

For instance, one of the elements in the task environment consists of the regulatory groups which set out the conditions within which the community may operate. For the housing co-operative the most important of such groups are governments which pass laws and regulations governing the operation of housing co-operatives: what their powers are, what financial and operational safe-guards they must abide by, the building by-laws, where they may build etc. And at this stage we may discover that though our earlier assessment of the social philosophy of our society is that it would welcome, or at least tolerate, the growth of a non-competitive, non-profit, co-operative community as distinct from housing schemes of a more conventional sort, the regulations concerning ownership, finances, etc., really make such co-operative communities very difficult, if not impossible, to get going. Housing legislation may be geared to the operation of private housing developers borrowing money at market rates from private sources of finance to build houses for individual owners, and it may, therefore, be necessary to go back to political action to have legislation introduced to make public money more easily available for low-cost co-operative ventures. This may involve a wide-ranging campaign of public education.

A second element in the task environment is that of the suppliers of resources – finance, land, labour, and materials. The first of these, finance, may be available from some of the regulatory groups referred to above. Land resources may be under the control or in the ownership of these same groups – state or municipal governments – or they may be available only from private landowners. Whatever these systems may be, they will affect the ability of the housing co-operative to attain its objectives.

A third element is the existing competitors, the alternative suppliers of housing. These include other housing co-operatives where the element of competition will lie in the standard and type of management offered by them, the degree to which they embody the spirit of community, the type of membership they cater for, and the type of housing offered. If the alternative suppliers of housing are private or public development schemes, the competition will come from the possible advantages of owning one's own house or apartment, or of being a tenant of a landlord who has to assume the responsibility for maintaining the property. The fourth element in the co-operative's environment is its potential members. I have suggested that there are different degrees of commitment to the idea of co-operative housing – to such things as communal laundry facilities, communally-used recreational space with a minimum of private garden, participation in management through a sort of town meeting. To all these elements the community constantly has to adjust, or be prepared to resist pressures to adjust, and possibly compromise its initial ideals.

BOUNDARIES

The boundaries of the system are delineated formally by the membership, but in reality they become fluid, or unstable, insofar as the system has to begin shifting and stretching its practices to maintain the interest and the interaction of members who begin to lose interest and show signs of opting out of active participation in the life and affairs of the system. For the boundaries of the system mark not just the formal or jurisdictional space of the system, nor just its physical space. They also mark its social space and the psychological commitment of members of the co-operative to its ideals and practices. The co-operative as a whole will have a social space vis-à-vis people outside the co-operative.

The question of boundaries is a difficult one to cope with in the more traditional idea of community as being something implicit in a population. Warren points out that a lack of accessibility of many problems to solution on a community basis, a lack of community autonomy, and a lack of identification with the community, are three barriers to the efficient mustering of forces to confront community problems (Warren 1963,19). The boundaries are thus more difficult to discern, and the function of boundary maintenance is more difficult to perform, where the space is primarily a psychological and social one without a clear jurisdictional space such as is demarcated by the membership of a co-operative. On the other hand, without a psychological and social space, even the fairly well identified and explicit system like a co-operative, is not a very stable or effective one.

INPUTS

The system's inputs are what is brought in from the task environment across the boundaries, to enable the system to do what it does and be what it is. We all belong at the same time to more than one group or system, and into each one we bring with us whatever it is in us which contributes to that system. In this sense, though the members of the housing co-operative are already within its boundaries, they are constantly bringing into it from their total being those qualities and talents in themselves which are relevant to this particular group. In other words, inputs are not only the physical or concrete things brought into the system, such as land, money, building materials, and equipment, but the talents and motivation of the members, and a flow of information which relates to the goals and the activity of the system. What is important to the co-operatives – and to all systems – and to their continued effectiveness is the degree of security, or dependability, of these inputs.

Take, for example, the motivation and talents of the members. I have already suggested that the boundaries of the system have something to do with the degree of commitment of members to the ideas and practices of the co-operative, and that there are other alternative and competing systems which may drain off some of this commitment. The economic concept of opportunity cost has something useful to say about this: members of the system will bring into it those talents and that degree of motivation for which there is a higher return, in terms of need-satisfaction, than if they were invested in some alternative system such as a privately-developed rental housing scheme. There is an opportunity cost attached to not belonging to that other system. One of the distinguishing elements of the community development approach is that it pays particular regard to the input into the community of the vaguely-measured and intangible interest, motivation, and talent of the members, and makes those inputs at least as important as the more concrete and material inputs that help to produce concrete and material outputs.

TRANSFORMATION

In terms of small group theory, which we discussed in the previous chapter, these intangible inputs are important elements in the maintenance function of group life, in the satisfaction of the social-emotional life of the members of the group. It is possible that even if the initial sense of commitment brought into the group by individual members is not very strong, it may be strengthened by the subsequent involvement of each member in the continuing life of the group. In the case of the housing co-operative this life consists of the meeting of, and interaction between, members in the process of planning and achieving the kind of housing which they set their minds on, and then on maintaining that housing in a state which meets their continuing needs. In terms of socio-technical systems theory, this process is called the transformation sector of the system. It transforms the system's inputs into outputs. The kinds of questions which consideration of the transformation sector allow us to ask of any community are as follows:

(a) What happens to information which is introduced into the system? How is it picked up and used? Does the system – in this case the co-operative – take adequate notice of information regarding the goals of the individual members, does it use that information in seeking to attain a group goal, or does it somehow lose it along the way? Does it make use of other information, e.g., about government regulations or sources of supply?

(b) What happens to the talents brought in by individual members? How are they used? Are they used in the best way possible, e.g., through a division of labour and through the establishment of some orderly process of planning, building, and management?

(c) How is the motivation of the members sustained?

(d) How are the financial and material inputs handled? Are they wasted or are they used in the most efficient way, i.e., to obtain the best results with the minimum of expenditure and consumption?

(e) How are all these inputs organized toward achieving the primary task of the co-operative?

Such questions again draw attention to both the maintenance and the task functions of the group. In enterprises which follow community development lines more concern tends to be directed to the social-emotional elements through maximum involvement of each member than is commonly the case in enterprises such as profit-making businesses, but an important part of the socio-technical systems approach, even as it is applied to businesses, is its insistence on the importance of both the social and the technical aspects of the enterprise. Where community development is concerned, it draws attention to the need to take into account not just the human element and the meeting of immediate human needs but also the technical apparatus within the system.

OUTPUTS

The socio-technical systems approach is also important in drawing attention to the importance of studying a system's outputs. The outputs are those products or services which relate to the goals of the system – but not only to these goals. The socio-technical systems model relates outputs to the goals of other systems in the task environment as well, so the outputs have this dual relevance. This element in the model is of particular importance in community development because it brings the community as I have defined it in this book into direct relationships with the wider society in which it exists. The community cannot be considered apart. In the case of the housing co-operative the outputs, seen from within the system and in terms of the systems goals, are the kind of housing which emerges and the kinds of relationships which come to exist between the people living there. Seen from outside the system, i.e., from the point of view of people and organizations outside the co-operative, the important outputs are the kind of housing, which must meet the goals of the government and local municipal authorities, including, for instance, the fire department and the public health department. But in a broader sense the outputs in terms of relationships between people living in the co-operative also have to meet the goals of the task environment in that the style of life in the co-operative must avoid offending the ideas and norms of the surrounding society at that time. For instance, excessive communitarianism – excessive in the eyes of the surrounding society – does not go well in most parts of North America, and it can bring to bear on the community pressures which may endanger its continued life.

A good, if extreme, example of the intolerance of a particular style of life on the part of a community by the surrounding society is shown in the fate of the Cold Comfort Farm Society in Rhodesia. The Society lived by the ideals of racial partnership; in the midst of the racially-segregated society of Rhodesia, Cold Comfort Farm was a community in which Africans and a few Europeans lived together and shared in decision-making, farming, and general living. The intolerance of such a philosophy and style of life on the part of the surrounding white society showed itself in harassment by the police over a period of years, and the eventual sequestration of the farm and all its property by the white government, their sale to a white farmer (all proceeds being kept by the government), the deportation from Rhodesia of some of the white members of the Society, and the dispersal of its African members (Clutton-Brock 1972).

Outputs can also be either intended or unintended; in other words, they may be in accordance with the original goals of the system or they may not be. An unintended output of the housing co-operatives might be a tendency of children in the community to consider every home as an open house for them to enter freely whenever they feel like doing so, with a consequent loss of privacy.

Systems variance is the extent to which, on the one hand there is a discrepancy between the fulfilment of the system's goals and those of other systems in the environment, and on the other hand there are outputs which are unintended and unacceptable and, therefore, not in line with the system's own goals. An examination of the system to discover if it is functioning satisfactorily begins at this point and goes on to study the transformation sector to see what causes the variance. This will indicate what interventions are advisable to improve the functioning of the system. The strategies by which interventions are to be made will be influenced by what is judged to be practical in the short and the long term.

ORGANIZATION DEVELOPMENT

Intervention techniques are emphasized in the literature on organization development in the United States. Bennis (1969,2), for example, defines organization development as a complex educational *strategy* intended to change the beliefs, attitudes, values and structures of organizations. Insofar as this refers to changing beliefs and values, it seems to go beyond the values which already exist in the organization, and this might be interpreted as changing the goals of the organization and consequently influencing outputs in the light of changed values and goals. In one sense this interpretation appears to be justified. In a short statement entitled 'What is OD?,' the NTL Institute for Applied Behavioral Science sets out some hypotheses underlying the theory and method of organization development, and these include the following: work which is organized to meet *people's needs* as well as to achieve organizational requirements tends to produce the highest productivity and quality in production; people have a drive toward *growth and self-realization* (NTL 1968; author's underlining).

In other words, these hypotheses suggest that in addition to the materialistic goals related to the production of goods and services, there should exist in an organization the goals of personal growth and of meeting the personal needs of people in the organization, which would seem to transcend production goals. This additional set of goals reflects the concern of the human relations movement and of such writers as McGregor, in his advocacy of a theory Y approach to management, in terms of which workers are seen not merely as unmotivated units of production but as persons who can contribute to the effective and efficient functioning of the organization if they are given the opportunity to do so (McGregor, 1960). Some of the outputs that go with such a set of goals are the creation of a feeling of trust among people in the organization, and an open, problem-solving climate of operations. In this sense, organization development might be said to envisage the possibility of substantial change in an organization.

In another sense, however, organization development does not seek to change the goals of the system. In fact, it is an important element of organization development practice to start with an examination of the goals of the system, whether they be profits from some form of production, or satisfactory housing for members of the system, or adequate health care facilities as in a hospital. And the aims of organization development as an educational strategy involve people's learning about those goals, becoming committed to them as part of their personal belief system, and helping to achieve them with minimum stress to themselves.

Looked at from the perspective of community development, and a more radical social philosophy, the actual practice of organization development as one can observe it in North America seems not to question goals at the deeper social level. Rather it accepts the values of the business world and seeks to make organizations more effective within that value system. The same can be said of many practitioners in human relations skills, whether they be group-process oriented or personal-growth oriented. It has become big business in itself, at hundreds of dollars a day, plus expenses, in consulting fees. In other words, the practice of organization development appears to accept the fundamental values inherent in the economic system, and it offers techniques for improving organizational effectiveness within that given framework.

In chapter 5 I suggested, in discussing the first model for analyzing the environment, that we have to start by taking into account the social philosophy and dominant values of the society in which we are working. But I also suggested there, and in chapter 2, the need to be examining critically the philosophy and values of our own western, industrial, competitive society in the light of new and old paradigms. And in this light we need to be critical of the acceptance that present organization development practice gives to the dominant values of our society and of the institutions that seek simply to perpetuate those values.

With this caution in mind, let us see what sort of process organization development involves:

(a) Identifying the problems facing the organization. This is the diagnostic, or scouting, phase.

(b) Setting problem priorities.

(c) Developing and sharing data concerning these problems – and these data may relate to technology, structure, and interpersonal and personal factors.

(d) Joint action planning, looking at various alternatives.

(e) The implementation and testing of selected alternatives.

(f) Periodic review and further action.

There appear to be two central tenets in this process. One is the value placed on choice – the ability and opportunity to discover and choose alternative ways of achieving a set of goals. It is an important part of the argument that there are more ways than one of doing this, and the somewhat mystifying term used for this is 'equifinality.' The more data that are made available to the relevant people in the system, the more choices of action become apparent, and the better the decisions are likely to be. The second tenet is that organization development is a continuing process. Both of these tenets are also characteristic of community development; data are shared by members of the community, the choice of alternative actions is then shared by them as well, and the development process is therefore a continuous one.

The actual techniques used in organization development to identify problems, develop data about them, and plan and implement action to meet them, are generally in line with the two hypotheses outlined above. They attempt to involve all relevant members of the organization and they pay regard to interpersonal and personal relationships and the need to create a climate of trust.

The collection of data is usually done by someone outside the organization – a 'disinterested' consultant – on the understanding that he will be authorized to reveal and discuss these data with the management of the organization. Ideally there should follow a confrontation meeting, at which members of the organization state and discuss the problems they face in doing the work they are expected to do, and they check their perceptions with one another and with the management. There may, for instance, be difficulties in interpersonal communication, so in order to reach a condition where people will be prepared to talk frankly in front of one another about their perceptions of how the organization functions, there may be a series of team-building exercises. If the collection and development of data about the organization reveals that one of the hindrances to effective operation is a lack of internal trust and communication, the T-group approach may be used to try to overcome this lack (Hampden-Turner 1970,chap. 7).

If the data reveal a lack of certain skills and knowledge required in the organization, then suitable training programs may be introduced, or certain staff members may be sent elsewhere for this purpose. If the existence of conflicting sub-groups is revealed, there may be sessions at which each group examines its perceptions of itself as a group and its perceptions of the other groups, and in a total group meeting these perceptions can then be compared, checked, and discussed openly. The skill involved on the part of the change agent or consultant is to know what techniques are appropriate in different situations, and how to introduce those techniques, and this skill is equally valuable for a change agent in a community, trying to help groups of people who form subsystems of the larger social system to become active and effective in social change. Both the general process and some of these techniques, such as the collection and checking of data, have important similarities to the stages of investigation of social conditions advocated and elaborated on by Paulo Freire in the creation of *conscientizacao* among oppressed social groups (Freire 1972,101-18). The Freire approach sets out to examine not only the internal condition of the community, but also the environment, and its values, in which the community exists.

In other words, organization development need not be a rigid model which sets down precisely each stage in a process of establishing or improving the efficiency of an organization or community. It is a way of proceeding to clarify issues and suggest further ways of tackling those issues; this is why it can be adapted for community development and used in a wider and more comprehensive sense than it is commonly used. This can be illustrated by a brief description of one exercise which I went through with an association of people in a small prairie city in Canada.

In a place like this, the centre of a prosperous farming region, the annual exhibition and agricultural fair has been an important element in economic and social life. But in recent years the methods of livestock raising and marketing in Canada have made livestock shows around which exhibitions and agricultural fairs have revolved, less relevant than in former years. The members of the exhibition association, therefore, wished to take a look at their present operations and future developments, and wished to have an outside consultant to guide them through such an exercise.

It seemed that the general lines of the organization development approach as set out above would form a suitable framework for the exercise. So the first step was to get the association to articulate the problems. This stage took the form of an all-day meeting of all the members of the association. After a preliminary discussion to clarify as far as possible the purpose and general expectations of the exercise, the members divided into groups, with flipchart materials, to set out their perceptions of the problem. After a time devoted to group discussion, each group came back and shared its perceptions with the whole gathering. And out of this stage emerged statements such as the following.

'There is a lack of common interests between the rural and the urban sections of the local population. The latter do not share the attachment of the former to livestock shows and the traditional type of fair.'

'There is a mutual lack of knowledge on the part of each section.'

'There is a lack of a sense of community.'

'There is not sufficient involvement by a wide sector of the people.'

'The image of the association is weak.'

In the course of this sharing of perceptions the differences between the two sectors, as they were represented within the association, came out, and were given some airing.

The next stage was to get the groups to go back and refine the problem by asking two questions: 'What is the situation now?' and 'What would we like to see?' The answers to these questions were then shared and discussed in the whole group, and in response to these questions the picture emerged that: the shows were competition- rather than people-oriented; government financial support was to be decreased for livestock shows; there were two communities in the city and its environs, one of which was interested in matters other than livestock; there was, nonetheless, in the association, a common feeling of pride in their shows and that some sort of annual event should be held, as promotion for the city as a good centre for economic, social, and recreational development; the two large cities in the province had moved away from annual exhibitions centred around livestock to a total entertainment/education/recreation event.

In the course of the group discussions and the subsequent general discussion, the split between the generally younger urban members – businessmen, lawyers, officials in school and other organizations – and the rural members, became clearer. The former were more openly talking about new directions and the latter, while intellectually conceding the need for these new directions, were evidently still not enthusiastic. What also came out was that the latter group comprised the majority of the association, had 'squelched' new ideas, and had not been enthusiastic to have this group experience held at all. By the end of the first day they were agreed to proceed to a similar meeting the following week, to look more specifically at solutions.

At the next week's meetings the small groups, and then the total group, discussed the forces which they perceived to be working in favour of and against the attainment of a new-style exhibition with a wider appeal and wider terms of reference. The forces against were boiled down to two: 'thinking from the old society' and 'no real theme.' The forces in favour were boiled down to: 'good location and good facilities,' and 'we are a centre of vacation land, winter and summer.' So, significantly, the resistance was still there, no clear new purpose had been agreed upon, and agreement about forces in favour of change were limited to physical and geographical features. The workshop ended with an agreement that a committee should canvass the citizens by questionnaire delivered to as many households as possible, asking for feedback about that year's exhibition and ideas for change, if any. This was subsequently done, and in the following year the association initiated an international folk festival, on the strength of the city's being a centre of an area with many ethnic groups. This has grown in recent years to become a provincial attraction.

In this case the consultant was external to the system. Bennis suggests that for the most part this should be so, and even in the case described above it is doubtful that there would have been quite as much open discussion if the process had been orchestrated by a member of the association.

However, increasingly in the theory and practice of organization development, attention is being paid to the role of the internal consultant, the person or group of persons who are designated within the system to review and take action with regard to unsatisfactory aspects of the operation. Such internal change agents are generally thought of as being legitimized, i.e., seen by others in the system as having this institutional role, and as being authorized to initiate change.

This is not, however, always so. Frequently the change agent may be legitimized as far as a sponsoring agency is concerned, but not as far as the community itself is concerned. A white community development officer working for the Rhodesian government, or for the Canadian Department of Indian and Northern Affairs, or a community relations officer in Britain, employed by a community relations committee, will be legitimized in the eyes of his employer but possibly not within the community in which he is working. In some cases a neutral, or sympathetic, community worker coming into a community, will – as in my own case in working with African groups – have to go through a period of trial and suspicion before being accepted and legitimized.

It is also recognized that there can exist within a system a non-legitimized change agent, a person or group of persons who are not seen as having any responsibility for initiating change, but are simply members of the system living or performing some function in it. The non-legitimized change agent is someone who senses a problem in the system and begins to be in conflict with others who do not perceive the problem or who perceive it in some different way. I referred in chapter 2 to a local issue in a community league in Edmonton, where the operators of two day-care centres pressed for the upgrading of the nearby children's playground. They had no standing in the neighborhood as change agents, but their objectives, their persistence, and their lobbying with members of the community league placed them in the role of change agents inside the community.

This question of non-legitimized internal change agents raises an interesting point about the relationship of a community to the wider society in which it is situated. There will be occasions – and, in fact, this is an important feature of community development in relation to broader social development – when a community performs the role of non-legitimized internal change agent with respect to the broader social picture. In Toronto, for instance, a group of environment-conscious citizens came together around the problem of the planning and constructing of a large freeway through the centre of the city – the Spadina freeway. This group attracted to it the support of such people as Marshall McLuhan. Eventually, after a long and vigorous campaign, they succeeded in having all construction on the freeway stopped, literally in its tracks. Another example is the recent establishment in a small town in a valley in the Canadian prairies, a town called Rosebud, of a community of artists – musicians, painters, and craftsmen – with the purpose of being a residential centre for the creative arts and the propagation of a philosophy of life based on sharing, creative (and economically profitable) production, and aesthetic awakening. After some initial suspicion on the part of the local people the centre is now obtaining their support and involvement, and is attracting to it young people wishing to participate. Findhorn, in Scotland, appears to be fulfilling a similar role and is beginning to attract world-wide attention.

The courses of action open to these three different kinds of change agent, the external consultant, the internal legitimized consultant, and the internal non-legitimized change agent, will be different. The first, and to some degree the second, will have available to them the opportunity to use the process and the kinds of techniques sketched out above, and their use of these techniques will, to a greater or lesser degree, be accepted by members of the organization. They may, in fact, run into resistance at some stage in the process insofar as significant members of the organization decline to take the risk of being too frank with other members, but they start with some degree of acceptance for their suggestions. Non-legitimized internal change agents enjoy no such initial acceptance, and their mode of operation has to be different. To begin with, they are confronted with certain psychological issues, such as their own self concept, and their capacity for taking risks in their relationships with their peers and for handling conflict within themselves and with others. To deal with these issues they have to develop appropriate strategies: to strengthen their self-concept, self-reliance, and tolerance of ambiguity and conflict; to seek a support group and to establish a wider identity within the system; to make themselves aware of options, by learning about the experience of others and about models and concepts appropriate to their case. This process of coping with the psychological issues which they face as individuals thus merges with the process of organization development, but the initial phases of this latter process cannot, as in the case of the legitimized change agent, take place in the open, with the approval of leaders in the system. The initial diagnosis or scouting, to clarify and articulate the problems of the system, as distinct from simply having a strong feeling that something is wrong in it, will consist of a discrete and unremarkable study of the formal goals and structure of the system, the informal goals and structure, the behavioural norms, the identity and the strengths and weaknesses of the formal and informal power figures, and the identity of the forces in the environment which affect the system. This need to be discrete, to act underground, places the non-legitimized change agent at a great disadvantage to the legitimized agent – external or internal. The non-legitimized change agent lacks the time and the opportunity to do this scouting; he has to be circumspect in identifying people in the system who will support efforts for change, and deciding with whom and at what point in time he can move toward openly identifying himself and mobilizing support – with whom, in organization develop-ment terminology, he is to make the initial contact.

In the sort of condition described by Paulo Freire, in other words in a system where the holders of power are concerned not with change but with maintaining the status quo, even the external change agent will, in terms of the larger system – likely be non-legitimized and will be seen as an *agent provocateur*. His legitimacy, insofar as he is accepted by the subsystem, or the community of the oppressed, is with that subsystem. In the United States, Saul Alinsky was a change agent acceptable to, and legitimized by, the groups with which he worked, but not with the larger social system in which those groups existed.

The concept of organization development can be applied to systems larger than businesses or housing co-operatives or hospitals. Beckhard is now applying it to what he calls large systems, and he goes so far as to include even whole nations within the possibilities of this type of analy-sis. He refers to four orders of social system: the individual; small groups such as the family; middle-sized organizations; the large institutions such as communities, nations, and the global system of the world.[1]

This discussion of organization development and socio-technical sys-tems theory has led us to the planning and decision-making stage of the community development process. Organization development, as we have seen, involves planning and implementing courses of action, and the socio-technical systems model helps us take proper account of the factors which will affect such action. But they have not examined in detail the actual process of reaching group decisions, and this is the purpose of the following chapter, which proposes a general model of group decision-making and some techniques to be used within that model.

---

1 Discussion by Richard Beckhard at the NTL Learning Community – Large Systems Module. Bethel, Maine, July 17-August 11, 1972

8

Problem-solving and decision-making

People have been solving problems, by changing their perceptual, behavioural, or cognitive skills (Kelley and Thibaut 1968,2) since the beginning, whether by trial and error, intuition, or logical thought. Changes occurring through serendipity – as in the Chinese fable about the first roast pig – are not problem-solving. In this fable, where the delights of roast pork are said to have been discovered when the pig sty burned down in the family's absence, they were not aware of what they were missing until they got it. A problem involves an awareness of a need to change; it is the way that people seek in order to effect such change.

Our progenitors, the apes, were solving problems before our time, and as Kohler has demonstrated, they go on doing it, as do mice in experimental mazes and pigeons in Skinnerian boxes. For problem-solving is a process of learning, whether in the stimulus-response mode or the cognitive/Gestalt mode. If we suggest that there are some who tend to act intuitively and spontaneously in ways that have particular relevance to community development – the community development artist, so to speak – all the more can we suggest that people have been able throughout history to get by in solving problems without knowing anything about problem-solving models.

There is a tendency to believe that problem-solving models, i.e., conceptualizations of the problem-solving process set to words or graphics or some other symbolic form, are some special production of recent years of research in the applied behavioural sciences. Having, in these more recent years, come into contact with some such models, I realize that a much earlier introduction to the art occurred for me when, as a young army officer in world war ii, I had impressed on me the mnemonic, 'Aye, Aye, Mac' – iimac: *Intention* – what do we intend to do? *Information* – what do we need to know in order to carry out our intention? *Method* – how are we going to carry out our intention? *Administration* – what supporting procedures, organizations, and supplies (of whatever kind) do we have to establish in order to support our method? *Consolidation* – what do we have to do to ensure that the gains we make are not lost? The questions seem appropriate whether the problem relates to an enemy gun position, a recalcitrant school board, or bad ghetto housing.

It is a frequent experience of those who work with groups of citizens, and even of professional workers, that they often seem to flounder, and become confused and frustrated, in some situations where they see a need for change but are not sure what it is. With groups concerned with the improvement of less easily defined conditions of life it often starts there: the initial problem is that they do not know what the problem really is. They know things are unsatisfactory – they are poor, or city hall does things which adversely affect them, or the young people are in revolt, and so on – but they do not know how to set about changing things. The problem in these three instances is not poverty, or city hall's decision-making or the revolt of the young. These are the *conditions* which give rise to the problem. The problem is to discover how to ameliorate poverty, to change the decision-making process, and to gain the co-operation of youth. And these problems do not have the clarity of those confronted typically by the military: to capture this, defend that, or destroy the other. The military model works on a principle which is valid in battle or in times of crisis, i.e., that there is not time to be taking a consensus of views. And this latter process is a feature of community development that distinguishes it from some other political processes.

This, by the way – for I do not propose to deal at any length with concepts of leadership – has something to say about styles of leadership in different situations. In conditions where broad questions of social morality and principle have been assumed to be answered and broad goals shared, i.e., where the problem has been broadly defined and agreed upon, and where time is pressing and actions have to be swift, acts of leadership are appropriate which are taken swiftly and without a process of consultation. Such a situation may well arise at particular times in the life of a community trying to conduct itself normally on democratic lines. But in general it is a negation of the community development process that problems should be defined and intentions declared for the community by some individual or clique either within or outside the community. Here the general style of leadership is one of helping the community arrive at a full understanding of problems and to share in the responsibility and procedure for solving them.

In effect, the whole of this book is about problem-solving, or arriving at ways in which groups of people can change conditions which they see as being adverse to them. And this chapter is the narrow end of a funnel, where all that has been put into the discussion so far comes to the point of action. This chapter cannot, therefore, be read without the earlier ones. The point of decision-making brings in all that has been said about learning and attitudes toward the nature of man, analyzing the environment, group processes, organizational processes, and the relationship of the group to its task environment. The models set out in the previous four chapters all relate to various stages of the process leading up to decision-making.

What this chapter does is to emphasize two things: (a) mainly, the need in community development to achieve group problem-solving, with some techniques which are appropriate to this need; (b) secondarily, in light of this, the limitations on problem-solving and decision-making in communities whose members are separated by distance and between whom personal contact is intermittent.

GROUP PROBLEM-SOLVING

In community development we are concerned with the solving of problems and arriving at decisions by groups, and not by individuals. As Friedmann suggests, direct engagement with society requires competence at the level of the group itself, but – as I have argued in chapter 3 – related to the larger enterprise of which it forms a part (Friedmann 1973,xviii).

I have said that it is a frequent experience of those who work with groups that the groups flounder when faced with situations which require the solution of a problem. In my own experience, I have sat for two days with a group of Indian alcoholism counsellors while they have tried to address themselves to their feeling of weakness and lack of support, and have tried to formulate, in that situation, the problem of establishing a supporting association. I have observed a strong and intelligent group of Junior League members who have struggled for months with the problem of how to make an impact on the decisions of city council on matters such as city parklands and housing renewal. I have experienced the frustration of a faculty council in its awareness of a lack of communication and cooperation between its members and its inconclusive attempt to tackle the problem of improving the situation. Such cases as these have shared the common feature of lacking a 'simple,' systematic approach to the problem.

And there is more to it. Attacking a problem as a group brings up the questions discussed in chapter 6, that is, openness and trust, interpersonal

TABLE 1

Process	Outcome
1 Become aware of existence of problem	1 Feelings of shared interests and goals
2 Group discussion to sharpen perception of problem in terms of group goals	2 Tentative statement of problem
3 Clarification of operational objectives, and how far these are now being met, or not	3 Establishment of a working definition of the problem
4 Preliminary search for solutions	4 Tentative list of solutions
5 Consideration of environment, resources, need priorities, and forces at work (screening)	5 Judgment on different solutions
6 Choosing one or more specific courses of action in the light of objectives and above considerations (decision-making)	6 Solution/decision
7 Evaluating the solution	7 Consultation in a quasi-state equilibrium

communication, and the formation of group perceptions. For when I suggested above that one of the problems is that the group does not know what the problem is, I was referring to the perception and awareness of the group as a whole. Within the group there are, no doubt, many individual perceptions of what the problem is, and even of the solution which should be sought. The process of problem-solving therefore has to begin there, with the multiplicity of perceptions in the group, and the initial phase of problem-solving has to be to bring this into a consensus.

So, not to state a blindingly new idea, group problem-solving starts with an awareness of a problem. This merges into the definition of the problem, by the group. It might seem excessive to go further and say that the problem does not exist until it is defined, but this seems to be true in an important sense. Take again the matter of poverty. Poverty in itself is not a problem: it is a condition. A range of problems is revealed in understanding what it is doing to people, and then what is to be done to stop it. Simply to do away with poverty, which is the lack of money and/other resources, may not be the solution of the problem. It is relatively easy to see this in the extreme case where the money is obtained by theft, but it is also possible to see it in the case where the money and other sources are

TABLE 2

Cognitive process	Central issue
1 Perceiving the nature of the problem (a) The existing condition is defined and the problem itself identified (b) The nature of the problem is investigated and its causes and effects rationally established	Does this condition really cause a problem? What makes this a problem?
2 Perceiving the relevance of the problem to oneself (a) The way in which the problem may apply to oneself is considered, both personally and as a member of a group (b) Its relative priority is examined	Is this our problem? How does it affect us? Is solving the problem a priority for us?
3 Perceiving the need to take the problem apart and resolve it (a) Further data needed to understand the problem is obtained (b) Alternative solutions are proposed (c) The relative merits and feasibility of alternative solutions are reviewed by the group (d) Decision as to the best course of action is taken individually or, where appropriate, as a group	 What can be done to resolve the problem? Which solution is best? What can we do as a group? What would we like to do individually? Or jointly? As a group?

provided as a form of dole. To provide even reasonably adequate welfare payments to whole populations of Métis colonies, and to do no more, does not solve the problems they face. These problems can only be revealed as the people can be brought, or can bring themselves, to think about the causes of their poverty and to understand how these may be addressed.

From there the process unfolds in a manner suggested in Table 1, adapted from Bloom, which relates stages of the process to outcomes arrived at during these stages (Bloom et al. 1956,121).

An alternative way of putting this, and at the same time underlining the previous point about the difference between a condition and a problem arising from that condition, is to outline a part of the strategy of problem-solving used in the Khit-pen literacy project in Thailand (Srinivasan 1977,32-22). It is shown in Table 2.

GOALS, OBJECTIVES AND DEFINITIONS

The first three stages of the process relate to the goals and objectives of the group. They express what has been emphasized from chapter 3 onward and will be further emphasized in chapter 9, that is, that the group's goals and intermediate objectives must be clear. The decision-making and action starts there. It is a common experience with groups that they often proceed straight to stage 4 of the process, or even stage 6, without having dealt adequately with stages 1 to 3. The above reference to poverty on Métis colonies can be used to illustrate this.

The solution to the condition of the Métis people, initiated by government and now accepted by many of the people themselves, is to provide welfare payments. This takes into account the condition of poverty, but does not address the problems, nor the goals of the people. The problems stem from numerous factors, e.g., the legal restrictions on the ownership of land in Métis colonies, with the consequent lack of a land-title base for borrowing; the history of being done to rather than being helped to do for themselves; all sorts of discrimination, legal and illegal, subtle and obvious, shown against native people; poor educational facilities; poor self-image. Becoming aware of and perceiving the problem in this way, on the part of both government and the Métis people themselves – along the lines described in the model of contemporary Indian culture in chapter 5 – begins the establishment of a working definition and possible solutions, e.g., revisions in land tenure provisions. The failure to look at the problems in this way for decades has aggravated the condition. The solution of welfare payments is no solution at all.

The early stages of the process of community development suggested in chapter 2 find a parallel in Upton's statement that problem-solving is an operation involving the problem-solver (knowledge, skills, attitudes in the group), his apparatus (organization, resources), and his environment. In the case of Métis development, none of these factors have really been properly taken into account. Upton goes on to point out that after making a tentative statement of the problem, we sort out data relevant to it in terms of some conceptual model (1961,15). In other words, we use conceptual models to choose, sort, and analyze information which we perceive to relate to the definition of the problem, one such model being the first one discussed in chapter 5.

THE SEARCH FOR SOLUTIONS

It is only after such a process of definition that we will be in position to proceed to the next step of seeking solutions and making decisions. The search may be in physical terms, or in terms of acquiring new perceptions, of forming new cognitions by the association of relevant information stored in the group memory (March and Simon 1958).

I discussed briefly this question of group memory in chapter 3. It is the store of knowledge, skills, and emotions which the group holds within itself, and with which it confronts new information that comes from outside. The group memory is thus a repertory of possible solutions to problems previously encountered, which may be appropriate to new problems (March and Simon 1958,117). New groups and groups inexperienced in the business for which they are formed have no memory in this sense. They are a summation of many individual memories, and in their new group life one of the processes they must go through is the reconciliation of the many individual memories into one group memory. Frequently, when only one of the group members has had previous experience of a problem similar to that which now confronts the group, this experience is accepted by the others as a basis for group action – an example of experience providing leadership.

On the other hand, the narrowing down of the group memory to a few members of the group, or on the extreme to one member, shifts the nature of the group to an oligarchy or dictatorship. The formation of a group memory can happen only as the group as a whole comes to share, through common experiences, the process of finding group solutions for group problems. In chapter 2, I drew attention to the long and groping process of the formation of a community, of all its members trying to know and trust one another and form common objectives, and part of that long process is this building of a group memory based on shared experiences. One word which is sometimes used in expressing the state of having attained such a group memory is 'morale.' The morale of a group, whether it be a military unit, a football team, or a community action group, is said to be high when the group has been through many experiences, has met them successfully, and has a feeling that, come what may, they have the ability to tackle it. Individuals have come to have confidence in their group, from past experience.

But the other aspect of problem-solving is innovation, that is, the formulation of fresh responses to challenging situations. And looked at from this aspect, the existence of a store of previous experience in the group memory can present some difficulties. March and Simon use the idea of sunk costs to explain such difficulties (1958,173). By sunk costs they mean the financial, physical, and psychological investment in the status quo. What we have now has cost us something; we have sunk money and/or labour and/or psychological effort into achieving what we have, and there may be a tendency to wish to stick with it. For to move on into new activities means breaking our attachment to the present state of things. Moreover, new activities will require the investment of fresh effort, in other words, costs of innovation. So there may be a tendency toward inertia. In the early stages of the community's life the sunk costs are minimal or non-existent. The trend of forces is toward change; the present condition is something from which the community wants to escape, so the costs of innovation are accepted as being less than those of remaining as we are. But as the life of the community proceeds, and some or many or all of those objectives are attained which were set out at the beginning, the investment in the past, in psychological terms, is increased, and so perhaps are the costs of innovation. On the other hand, the experience of reaching these objectives may have moulded the community into a group with a high morale and a smooth and efficient working system, and this will tend to reduce the costs of innovations. At this point the community may begin either to stagnate, resting on its past investment, jealous of what it has sunk into its existing condition, or to formulate new objectives and begin to work toward them with the strength it has gained from past successes. So the needs of innovation are served not by a commitment to past experience, but by reordering the elements of that experience into new patterns. An innovation is an element newly introduced into a given situation. (Friedmann 1973,103). Innovation is not a complete escape from experience, for that is impossible; it is the restructuring of the element of experience. In terms of Gestalt learning theory, it is the creation of a new Gestalt, switching the figure and the ground and seeing how it looks from there.

SEARCH TECHNIQUES

A technique available to groups in this search stage of problem-solving is brainstorming. When there is sufficient understanding of and agreement about the problem and sufficient conciseness rather than generality, it is then possible to set about accumulating possible solutions to the problem which can be sorted and judged in the light of their practicality. When a group has been able to specify a problem, brainstorming is a process of meeting together in one place for relatively short periods of time – not more than an hour at one time – and proceeding to let the members of the group churn out ideas for solving the problem – storming the problem, as Osborn (1961,84) has called it. During this process four basic rules apply:

(a) Criticism is ruled out, i.e., adverse judgment of any of the ideas must be withheld until later. (b) 'Free-wheeling' is welcomed, i.e., the wilder the idea the better. 'It is easier to tame down than to think up.' (c) Quantity is wanted – the more ideas the better. (d) Combination and improvement are sought, i.e., members of the group not only produce their own ideas, but build on those of others.

Brainstorming is therefore based on the principle of suspended judgment, of separating the process of producing ideas from that of analyzing and judging them, which comes later.

Osborn suggests that the ideal size of each brainstorming group is about a dozen, but he refers to groups of as many as 150 which, under practised leadership, have been successful in producing a great many ideas in a short space of time. A feature of the technique which has a particular bearing on community development is that it admits that people who are not so-called experts in the question being discussed are capable of having good and original ideas about it. It is being used by professional and business organizations and by citizens and neighbourhood groups. On the other hand, experimental work on this technique of problem-solving indicates that small numbers, and particularly pairs, are most effective. It also indicates that the value of the technique depends on relations between members of the group, and the type of leadership (Kelley and Thibaud 1968,73).

While research in this field appears to indicate that for producing ideas group brainstorming is superior to the efforts of individuals acting independently, other group techniques have been suggested as superior to brainstorming (Van den Ven and Delbecq 1971,203-12). In fact, it is suggested that certain features of brainstorming inhibit creative thinking – covert judgments may not be expressed openly for fear of ridicule; low-status group members may feel inhibited; group pressures may lead to conformity; etc. An alternative technique called the nominal group process permits group members to engage in individual reflection and search and to note down ideas without pressure, before such ideas are pooled. Delbecq and Van den Ven (1971) describe a process which they have used in a variety of situations and which incorporates this technique of nominal group process. Hall and Dixon have described yet another technique, which they call cybernetic sessions, for generating and gathering ideas in moderate-sized and large groups (Hall and Dixon 1974).

These are becoming increasingly sophisticated techniques for both defining problems and seeking solutions, and a movement in this direction of expertise and sophistication suggests a danger in the field of consulting and group facilitating that Friedmann criticises in the general field of planning. He suggests that the two modes of behaviour, one (the expert) oriented to the acquisition of knowledge, the other (the actor) to the acquisition of power, seem to be growing farther apart. Problems are formulated in ways that men of action do not understand. This is another way of seeing the increasing centralization of decision-making at the national level which I refer to in chapter 3 in discussing group memory. The practice of surrounding the prime minister with non-elected experts isolates the elected members of parliament, and the other career officials, from the making of decisions and initiating of action, so that the latter come to a point of not understanding. In more local affairs the proliferation of consultants in various sorts of economic and social planning and community action isolate the community members from the process, so that they also come to not understand.

Friedmann (1973,111) suggests that the solution lies in the adoption of a transactive style of planning – forging a personal relationship between expert and client actor. In this Friedmann is half-right. From the community development point of view what is even more important is a greater sharing of expertise.

SCREENING AND SELECTING SOLUTIONS

At the next stage the element of practicality is introduced. In Upton's terms, this means considering the ideas in terms of the people themselves, i.e., the problem-solvers, of the apparatus at their disposal, and of the environment. In terms of the first model referred to in chapter 5 it means considering them in terms of: (a) the social philosophy, i.e., what is acceptable to the group in terms of its own value system and to the larger society and its value system; (b) the social structure, i.e., the institutions in the society which may aid or hinder the attainment of what is contained in the suggestions; (c) the resources available to the group; (d) and the needs of the group in order of priorities.

What is happening at this stage is the making of decisions on what should and can be done, and the order in which it should be done. It may be decided that a series of objectives, from short-term to long-term, should be set for the whole group together, or a number of objectives should be set for smaller sub-groups (they may be called *ad hoc* working committees) to work toward simultaneously, all in terms of a general group objective. The components of the problem are being organized, and the process of programming is beginning to take place.

For this stage of the process one of the best-known techniques is that suggested by Kurt Lewin: force field analysis. The features of this type of analysis arise out of Lewin's interest in group dynamics in the late 1930s and during the second world war. One of his germinal articles setting out the basis for the development of the idea was entitled 'Frontiers in group dynamics' (1947). The basis of such analysis lies in the concept of the social field, or life space, which is the sum of 'the relevant physical and social facts in one's surrounding,' and the resultant forces that play on one. What happens within such a field depends upon the distribution of forces throughout the field. Where groups are concerned, these forces include 'group goals, group standards, group values and the way the group sees its own situation and that of other groups' (ibid., 12). The social field of the group, i.e., its structure and its ecological setting, are characterized by the relative positions and values of these forces and the physical entities in the field. Moreover, the relative position of all these entities expresses the possibilities of locomotion within the field, i.e., where and how the group is likely to move.

Lewin, and other writers who took up his method, distinguish between driving forces, i.e., those which tend to support the movement toward a goal, and restraining forces, i.e., those which tend to impede such movements. One asks what forces keep the group in its present groove (Jenkins 1964,23). And the phase of programming, or planning solutions, is one of asking how such forces are to be tackled in order to obtain movement away from the present situation toward the agreed goal. Jenkins states it in the form of a number of questions: (a) What forces, if any, must be dealt with before change can occur? (b) Are there some forces whose direction can be reversed? (c) Which restraining forces can be reduced with the least effort? (d) Which driving forces can be increased?

The present position is where the sum of the driving forces and the sum of the restraining forces are equal, and thereafter the analysis of ways to solve the problem, achieve change, and attain the goal follows the line indicated by the questions set out above. And in order to ensure change it is suggested that emphasis must be placed on the reduction of the important restraining forces. Leaving these forces untouched is likely to lead to an unstable condition in which they may push us back to where we were, as if they were springs pushed tighter, ready to shoot back if they should get the chance. In other words they are still there, unresolved. Lewin makes the important point that it is possible to increase the strength of the opposing forces on both sides without moving from the present position, and that the result is an increase in tension, or in the degree of conflict (Lewin 1965,434). This is a common experience, where attempts by one group to pressure an opposing group, with no sensitivity to the reasons for that other group's stand and no attempts to diminish them, do not forward the cause of either group, but increase or create conflict between them in a position of stalemate.

This process can be illustrated by referring back to the example outlined in chapter 7 – the exhibition association of the western Canadian prairie town. There the existing situation was that they operated a fairly successful annual livestock show and agricultural fair, that the show was competition-oriented and not people-oriented, and that it revealed and reinforced the existence of two communities, the rural people and the urban people. After a preliminary study of the problem the members of the association perceived their objective to be an on-going series of activities, including an annual exhibition, which would entail the participation of more urban residents. They then set out their perceptions of the forces which would favour and those which would impede the attainment of this objective, and these appeared as follows: *Forces for*: many dedicated community people; people with new ideas; new capital development plans; good geographical locality; energetic board of directors; quality and quantity of stock; ability of stock exhibitors; availability of other town facilities. *Forces against*: some people still thinking in terms of old agricultural show; antiquated grandstand and barns; limited long-term financing; tradition; poor contact with downtown business; no real theme; duplication of events in town; non-involvement of people from neighboring centres.

These forces were refined down by the group to what they saw as being the most important on both sides, which were as follows. *Forces for*: good location of show grounds; good geographical position as a centre. *Forces against*: thinking from the old society; no real theme.

The actions which the group arrived at as promising a reduction of the restraining forces were: (a) to begin working on the concept of a year-round program of events; (b) to break down the one large show committee into other working committees; (c) to spread contacts to other organizations; (d) to encourage participation from outlying areas; (e) to hold a competition for a theme; (f) to get public feedback through a questionnaire to be delivered to as many households as possible; (g) to maintain the existing high motivation and commitment of association members.

One refinement of this technique is to consider the forces at work under three headings: forces in the situation, forces in the group, and forces in the leaders. Forces in the situation include the social philosophy, tradition, social structure of the environment, the goals of other systems in the environment, the available resources and lack of resources – financial, physical, climatic, etc. Forces in the group include the group memory, i.e., the level of knowledge and skills of its members in relation to the objectives, the degree of specialization and how it is organized, the cohesion of the group, the interpersonal relationships, and the group's ability to work together. There will also be the important element of the group's traditions or lack of them. The forces in the leader may relate to the identified formal leaders or to the informal leaders. At one level of community work the needs of leadership may be as simple as knowing how to chair a meeting, or take minutes, or keep simple accounts; at another level they may involve complex administration and/or subtle politicking. They will always include the right personality to attract the trust of other people. The focus may be diffused or be centred on one or a few formal leaders; leadership may be a function of many members of the group, being exercised in different ways at different times. In other words, the exercise of leadership will be related closely to the forces in the group.

According to Lewin, telling people what to do involves increasing the driving forces, while getting people to participate as a group in analyzing a problem involves reducing the restraining forces. Lewin himself quotes the results of experiments with groups of Red Cross volunteers, in getting them to increase the use of beef hearts, sweetbreads, and kidneys during world war II, and with groups of mothers in getting them to use orange juice and cod liver oil in feeding their children (1965,427-32). In these cases the group discussion method proved more effective than lectures in achieving changes in behaviour. Similar experiments, with the same general results, have been reported by E.B. Pelz (1965,437-44). Since those relatively early days, the force field analysis technique has been used widely in problem-solving by community groups and in organization development.

The stage of choosing a solution becomes the means of achieving the objectives determined earlier in the process. Assuming this to have been done, the final step is to consolidate, or ensure that the chosen solution is not undone, and the outline of the force field analysis has indicated that one important requirement is to try to ensure that the forces which resisted the attainment of the objective are removed or sufficiently lessened so as not to push the group back. In other words, the consolidation of the objective does not begin only after the objective has been reached, but has to be prepared for during the problem-solving and action stages. In terms of the military model referred to earlier in this chapter, consolidation will be achieved only if the method and administration have been properly carried out. But even then, what is attained is what Lewin calls quasi-stable equilibrium, where for a time the strength of the forces tending to move the group to its objective are equal and opposite to those tending to move it back from the objective. The consolidation of the objective is not forever: new tensions arise, new problems, and new forces, which initiate a new cycle of learning and change.

If consolidation is to take place on the basis of the solution which provides the means to attain the agreed objectives, this means that the solution has to be evaluated. Does it, in fact, achieve what we set out to achieve? This brings us to a discussion of evaluation in community development, in the following chapter.

The decision-making process outlined above requires a good deal of group work, where people in the process are in close touch with one another for at least part of the time. This requirement places a limitation on the effectiveness of communities and networks whose members are separated by distance and between whom contact is intermittent. Communication through long range media such as telephone, television, and the mails has therefore to be supplemented from time to time by personal contact. It means that for crucial parts of the action and of the development process as a whole in such communities, people have to come together, and insofar as this does not happen the action will be less effective. It is a matter of what Friedmann calls the life of dialogue in a planning process – the personal meeting and entering into a co-operative and synergetic relationship (Friedmann 1973,183).

There are two aspects or phases of the decision-making and action process in community development. One is agreement within the community about such elements and processes as those proposed by Loomis and discussed in chapter 3: goals, beliefs, sentiments, norms, status-roles, ranks, power, sanctions, facilities, communication, and boundary maintenance (Loomis 1960,8). If this agreement is present, and members of the community share a commitment to them, then the second phase of decision-making can take place, which is the process described in this chapter. And with such agreement this can take place within a smaller sub-group of the community, even where the community as a whole may be spread out over a wide geographical area. The subgroup will be able to arrive at decisions within the context of the commonly agreed elements of the system, the authority to do so having been given to it by the wider community. And it will retain this authority so long as its decisions are seen by the community to fall within the framework of the generally agreed elements and processes.

The first phase of the process, i.e., the agreement on basic elements and processes, covers the early stages of the model of community development discussed in chapter 2: the identification of the problem, the learning about the group and the environment, the groping for community identity, the formulation of objectives, the establishment of organizational procedures. It is in this process that agreement is reached on the elements and processes of the community. The second phase, decision-making and action, then follows. For example, the Indian Association of Alberta was formed out of the feelings of tension and frustration of the Indian people of Alberta about their conditions. Its members spent a long time initially debating among themselves, having meetings, formulating policies, electing representatives to a central board, setting up an administrative machine. While this was going on (and it will be constantly recurring as the environment changes) some false steps were taken by the central board of the Association – false in the sense that they did not meet the expectations of the people. As the community gathered internal strength and settled down, the board could become more confident of having the authorization of the membership of the Association in making decisions.

But two dangers have to be avoided. The first is that the network of communication between all members of the community shall not be allowed to fall apart, because then the commonality of elements and processes (goals, values, norms, etc.) gets lost and decisions are made by the subgroup without validation by the total community. This is what Mao Tse-Tung meant by democratic centralization and 'from the masses to the masses.' In an organization like the Indian Association one does in fact hear from time to time criticism from people living on the reserves about decisions and behaviour of board members and officials as being in accord not so much with what the people want, as with what the officials presume. The 'experts' become isolated from the 'doers.'

The second danger is that with its membership spread out geographically the subgroup itself begins to be less coherent. Decisions are made without the full group participating. The dialogue that Friedmann refers to ceases, misunderstandings and disagreements occur, and dissention affects the community's effectiveness.

The general model of the problem-solving and decision-making process set out in this chapter includes as its final stage the evaluation of the decision arrived at, and the consolidation of the quasi-stable equilibrium which results. It is the purpose of the following chapter to examine in more detail the process of evaluation in community development.

9

Evaluation in community development

Once, in a graduate course in community learning, it was agreed that the final standing of each student would be evaluated on a number of factors, such as observation studies and a class presentation; that each student would assess his or her own mark on this basis; that the two instructors would independently make their own evaluations; and that the instructors and each student would discuss and compare their marks at the end. One student, who had performed with no particular enthusiasm or distinction, assessed his mark as nine, on a nine-point scale. When asked on what basis he made such a favourable evaluation, he said, 'Because I feel good about myself in this course.'

This is not to deny the validity of feelings in evaluating the results of one's actions, but the feelings must, for such purposes, be of the kind described by Pirsig's hero in *Zen and the Art of Motorcycle Maintenance* – the feeling, or peace of mind, that is produced by good workmanship; 'the everyday understanding of the shop,' on the part of the craftsman who knows that the work is well done, and knows that the motorcycle knows (1975,290). In Jungian terms, perception must be supported by judgment (Jung 1923; Mogar 1969,19-23). In Pirsig's terms, the romantic needs its complement, the classical. For community development is not a matter of inner ecstasy, but of outward and visible manifestations of human well-being on the part of the members of the community. Neither is, in itself, good enough. It is a question similar to that which poses the stringent methods of experimental research, with its controlled variables and manipulated situations, against the open-ended methods of clinical practice. Work in community development can benefit from both the results of experimental research and the flexible skills of good clinical practice.

For community development, besides being a concept informed by certain political and social values, is a way of doing things. It is a social practice. Its evaluation must therefore be of practical use. Research that is part of the development process cannot hold some elements constant and neutral (if this is ever really possible), while taking account of and manipulating others. We are concerned with living people in a changing situation.

There are three main reasons why evaluation in community development must have a practical purpose, i.e., must get at more than vague expressions of good feeling about outcomes. First, community development involves effort by people in a community – their active participation through the expenditure of time, energy, and sometimes financial and physical resources. It is therefore important that these people should have some idea of what they are getting for their effort, and that they should not come to feel that they are simply material for someone else's purposes. One recalls the complaint of so many community groups, including north American Indian tribes and bands, of being surveyed to death by social scientists to no discernible purpose.

The second reason is one which some people would argue vitiates the whole philosophy of community development by subordinating it to the expediencies of formal government. Community development in terms of the work of an agency, or of agency workers, usually involves the resources of some outside authority, government or non-government, which sooner or later is likely to require an accounting for the use of such resources. There are many references in the literature to this problem, and to the relationships and tensions between community development services and other government departments competing for scarce government resources (Du Sautoy 1964, Mezirow 1963, Mukerji 1967). In the province of Alberta in Canada – to give a specific example of the realities which community development workers have to cope with – we have had the case where after a few years of operation the provincial community development service was reorganized to bring it under the authority of an official with a more orthodox administrative background, and later under the general umbrella of a government co-ordinating authority.

A third reason for evaluation is suggested by Lewin. In a field that lacks objective standards of achievement no learning can take place. Unless we can judge whether an action has led forward or backward, and unless we have criteria for evaluating the relation between effort and achievement, there is nothing to prevent us from making the wrong conclusions. 'Realistic fact-finding and evaluation is a prerequisite for any learning' (Lewin 1948,202).

To many community development and people-oriented workers the kind of control involved in research to evaluate projects or programs is a negation of the whole concept of human development. There is a feeling implicit in the attitude of the student quoted above, that research of any sort in this field is ineffective, inappropriate, and/or insulting to the people involved. This feeling is partly a reaction against the kind of 'objective,' 'impartial,' quantitative data-collecting involved in so much psychological and sociological research, which is said to dehumanize the people who are subject of the research. It is also a reaction, on the part of some, to the quantitative, norm-referenced form of teaching and testing that permeates the formal education system. It amounts to a reaction against what is seen as an excessive intellectualism and a purely analytical approach to human development and learning.

But the counter-reaction on the part of governments, some social scientists, and funding agencies, to this insistence on freedom to be and to act without evaluation and accountability is a reality which community development enthusiasts have to deal with. It also appears to be justified where the resources being used are provided by others who face competing and honorable demands for such resources. There are signs, even among humanistic social scientists, of a re-examination of the possible excesses involved in this affective 'soft' approach to learning and human development. (May 1971; *Journal of Human Psychology* 1971). What is needed, therefore, is sensitive attempts to find appropriate measures of whatever it is we are aiming at. And in community development an important aim must be to enable the people involved to take part in establishing these measures and using them.

ACTION RESEARCH

Evaluation in community development must therefore be a process carried out in an effort to assess, through the use of relevant indicators, what development, if any, is resulting or has resulted from whatever program, action, or other input has been brought to bear on the community (either from within, or without, or both). In these terms evaluation is applied research, with the practical purpose of improving our knowledge of the nature of the change and development which we are concerned with from time to time in specific communities. In Lewin's words, it is a type of 'action-research, a comparative research on the conditions and effects of various forms of social action, and research leading to social action. Research that produces nothing but books will not suffice' (Lewin 1948,202-3).

Action research, Lewin suggests, is a cycle of planning, execution, and reconnaissance. At the planning stage a general idea is formed, it is examined in the light of fact-finding related to the idea, an over-all plan is formulated, specific objectives are worked out, and initial action steps are decided upon. The action steps are then taken, i.e., the execution stage is carried out. Then a reconnaissance is made to see how and to what extent the action has resulted in the accomplishment of the objective. Following the reconnaissance a new cycle of planning, execution, and reconnaissance begins. And a point of importance in community development is to have the community authorize the research and participate in its continuance and utilization (Biddle and Biddle 1966,chap. 8).

A further definition of action research is as follows: 'An on-going study of a social process and its results to date, which is carried on as part of the process. The accumulated findings are used to guide and correct the decisions of the continuing process. Participants contribute to research in the manner that their increasing ability allows' (Biddle and Biddle 1966,128).

Such a definition helps to avoid a tendency toward an excessively loose and permissive interpretation of social change, which turns it into a justification for action with very little, if any, research. To be useful for the people who are said to be involved in it, action research requires not only action, but also the means of examining that action and comparing the original state of being with successive states of being as action proceeds. In other words, what development is really taking place?

The concept of action research has been carried further in recent years in the discussion on participatory research, and the questioning of the appropriateness of the 'objective' research methods of the natural sciences to human affairs. In Husen's (1974,122) words, applied to education but appropriate to the evaluation of all human development, 'the use of a certain "method" in teaching must not – and cannot – be equated with use of a certain fertilizer.' Hall (1975) suggests seven principles underlying participatory research, which echo Lewin's views and take them further, in the light of the work and opinions of such people as Freire. (a) Research methods have ideological implications. (b) A research process should be of some immediate and direct benefit to a community and not merely the basis of an academic paper. (c) A research process should involve the community or population in the entire research project from the formulation of the problem to the discussion of how to seek solutions and the interpretation of the findings. (d) If the goal of the research is change, then the research team should be composed of representatives of all elements in the situation that have a bearing on the change. (e) The research process should be seen as part of a total educational experience which serves to establish community needs, and increase awareness and commitment within the community. (*f*) The research process should be viewed as a dialectic process, a dialogue over time and not as a static picture from one point in time. (*g*) The object of the research process, like the object of the educational process, should be the liberation of human creative potential and the mobilization of human resources for the solution of social problems.

An example and explanation of an attempt to apply such principles in the field is given in the account of an evaluation of the Integrated Family Life Education Project in Ethiopia in 1975, 1976, and 1977 (Crone 1977). Criteria for 'success,' and a data feedback system, were devised with the participants in the project. An external evaluation in 1977 found that the reason for the program's widespread acceptance by the people was the people's involvement in the planning, operations, and feedback process.

INDICATORS OF DEVELOPMENT

I have referred above to the use of relevant indicators to assess what development, if any, takes place. These indicators appear to have two dimensions. One relates to change which is visible and even tangible – changes in the physical and economic state of the people in the community, the amenities they enjoy, the material resources at their disposal. The other relates to the attitudes, self concept, personality, and relationships of the people in the community. These two dimensions bear a close relationship to two approaches to community development which some see as alternatives, and not complements, about which endless argument has taken place among people involved in community development, namely, community development as a matter of *projects*, producing tangible results such as roads, electricity, clinics, etc., or a *process of personal and social growth*, producing new attitudes, new resilience, new optimism. It is surely both, and one of the purposes of embarking on community development research should be to enable us to get clearer in our minds what results we are aiming at in each community development program. In other words, what is the objective? And by what criteria can we assess that the objective has been achieved?

EDUCATION MODELS

There are some concepts and models in the field of education which can be applied to community development research in order to answer such questions.

First, there are the criteria suggested by Lumsdaine (1965) for evaluating an instructional program. They are, its *appropriateness*, its *practicality*, and its *effectiveness*. Since the first and last of these criteria require a clarification of objectives (appropriate and effective in relation to what?) it is important to return for a moment to this crucial question of objectives. The educational model from which these criteria are borrowed states objectives in terms of behaviour or products of behaviour on the part of the individual learner. I have just suggested that relevant indicators of development are of two dimensions – physical and material things, and personal and social growth. A judgment about the realization of physical and material objectives, and an articulation of such objectives, are reasonably easy to make. Behaviourists would go further and claim that personal and social growth, like concepts such as 'feeling,' 'sentiment,' etc. are conjectural in themselves and can be judged only through observable behaviour (Skinner 1971,15). Like Mead, I agree with this behaviourist view in the sense that social psychology starts with an observable act, while not ignoring the inner experience of the individual (Mead 1934,7). I accept the criticism by people like Erasmus of the tendency among many community development enthusiasts to see it all in terms of the good feeling and good relationships of the people who are being 'helped' (Erasmus 1968). For in the end such feelings and relationships, such a sought-for state of affairs, can be judged only in terms of how these people behave: what the level of alcoholism is, how they work together, how they come to decisions, how they solve problems as a group. Community development is not a matter of inner ecstacy. This is a theme which must recur throughout, and it has to be emphasized that whether the objectives are seen in terms of physical things, material standards, or psychological and social states, they must be thought out carefully and expressed with the least ambiguity, so that at the end of the action we can see how far we have met them.

The *appropriateness* of a program is a matter of the relationship between its objectives and, on the other hand the needs of the people, and on the other hand the goals of the agency. Here I use the term 'agency' to embrace the individual consultant or community development worker and/or the organization which either employs such a worker or acts collectively in a community-based issue. These three factors have to be made clear initially. First, what are the objectives of this program, or project, or series of activities? Then, how do these objectives fit with the needs of the community? Then, how do they fit with the nature of the agency? These appear to be questions of common sense, but I would guess that anybody with experience in community work could think back and find a number of instances where these questions were not asked, or were not answered. The one which tends particularly to be glossed over is the third – the relationship between program objectives and the nature and goals of the agency, and very importantly, of agency workers as people. There are two different questions involved here. The first is that of the agency as a whole. It has happened that voluntary organizations which become involved in community work, having had a social need brought to their notice, have been tempted to assume and cling to programs beyond their competence, while there already exist other competent agencies in that particular field. The frequent result is a failed project and all sorts of rationalizations, and even denials, of failure. Likewise, there are occasions, for example among Canadian Indians, when it has been more appropriate for a government department to permit and facilitate the engagement of a non-government agency in a program than to undertake the program itself. A second question is that of the integrity and competence of the individual community workers. This refers not only to the frequent debate about generalists and specialists, i.e., when to know the need for a general co-ordinating role or a specialist technical role; it goes deeper than that. It seems important for a worker to bear in mind his own needs, personality, and integrity, and not to be constantly ignoring or even submerging these in the face of demands from others, thus tearing himself apart in the process.

The *practicality* of the program relates to the demands it makes on the resources of the community and of the change agency. If money is needed, how much, and where can we get it? What other resources are needed, and are they obtainable? There are many ways of answering such questions, depending on resourcefulness, ingenuity, skill, and optimism, and upon the sort of analyses which are possible by using the models discussed in earlier chapters of this book, but the point here is that there have to be answers in order to be able to decide whether the program is likely to be worth even beginning.

Consideration of the third criterion, *effectiveness*, serves to introduce another instructional model which can be adapted to the purposes of community development. This model suggests a procedure for the assessment of effectiveness, and it comprises the following elements: objectives, pre-assessment, or initial diagnosis; design of program, or process to be followed; monitoring and assessing, or measuring achievement; revision (Glaser 1965, 771-809).

We are back again with the crucial matter of objectives. Whatever model or technique we are working with – learning model, systems model, force field analysis, etc. – we are brought back to this need to begin with a clear statement and understanding of objectives. Otherwise, as far as research and evaluation are concerned, we do not know what we are evaluating.

Following the determination of objectives, pre-assessment is an attempt at the beginning of a program to get a reasonably accurate idea of where the people in the community are in relation to the objectives. How do they behave at the present time in relation to what appears to be the problem? If the objective is to achieve a functioning community recreation program, what is the present situation regarding recreation? If the objective is to achieve a 25 per cent increase in average incomes in the community, what is the present income level? For research purposes the more accurately this initial condition can be recorded, the better.

One again becomes aware of the difficulty related to an objective stated in terms of personal and social growth. How does one pre-assess and record an initial condition related to an ultimate objective of social integration, or of healthy individual self-concepts? What measuring instrument does one use? And since a vital element in community development is the engagement of the people in the community, how will such engagement be affected by an attempt on the part of community development workers or social scientists to go around at the outset asking people to subject themselves to questionnaires, surveys, etc.? There are two ways in which to approach these types of questions. One is the collection of what information is available in demographic and economic statistics and any other external data from which inferences may be drawn. But these will still leave us at the surface of people's experience. To get inside that experience, to get people to be open so that we can understand and express in more depth the human situation from which we start and to which we progress requires the participation of the people in the assessment and the subsequent action, i.e., participatory research methods, referred to earlier. What this means is that the design of the whole program must involve not only social science methods, but also the people who use them, and those to be subjected to them. The important thing is to enable the pre-assessment, and the subsequent assessments, to be made in as natural a condition as possible.

Popham and Baker (1970), in discussing behavioural indices for assessing achievement in instruction, suggest two kinds of index – a product index and a behaviour index. The product index is something the learner produces, such as written answers to test questions, or a painting, or, for a group, a tangible product such as a community hall. A behaviour index is an observable way of behaving, such as the regularity of getting up at sunrise to go out to work, or high attendance at meetings, or a lower incidence of alcoholism in the community. Popham and Baker suggest that there are two ways of obtaining these indices, by manipulated conditions, and by natural conditions. An example of a manipulated condition is an examination arranged in a set room at a set time, or the setting of a battery of personality tests. A natural condition is one in which the learner is observed, or produces whatever he is learning to produce, in his own natural surroundings.

It is suggested, even for more formal kinds of learning, that the collection of data under normal conditions is better than under manipulated conditions. In community development there is even stronger reason to ensure as natural a condition for data-gathering as possible. Whether the indices for assessing change are to be product or behaviour will depend on the change-objectives, on how involved the people in the community are in the data-collecting, what their views are, and to what extent the design of the program provides for them to be helped to observe and record their own behaviour, as individuals and as groups.

A good example of the process of community involvement in data collecting and in the recording of indices of assessment is provided in the 'Challenge for Change' program run in some of the Newfoundland outports by the Department of Extension, Memorial University, Newfoundland, and the National Film Board of Canada (Henaut 1971-2). Here records of community discussion at various stages were obtained by video-tape, operated by community members, for subsequent feedback to the community. This technique has since been carried further in Canada under the sponsorship of the University of Calgary in the Drumheller area of Alberta (Karch 1971-2), and under the sponsorship of the University of Saskatchewan in the Moose Jaw area of that province.

In these examples, behaviours and achievements are recorded visually and can be kept in that form. What is of prime importance is that accurate and honest records should be kept, in whatever form will provide a measurement of good management and effective operations. Whatever money is concerned – particularly but not only where the money is being provided by outside agencies or people – good management is measured partly through accurate financial accounts, of greater or lesser sophistication; so these are one requisite. Another is accurate and sufficient recording of meetings at which decisions are made. Where the objectives are, for instance, a lower incidence of alcoholism in the community, indices have to be identified for recording progress.

This is a very real and present need among Alberta Indians who are tackling one of the most serious problems on their reserves – alcoholism. A system of native alcoholism counsellors has been set up in the province by the Indians themselves, in which such counsellors – most of whom are ex-alcoholics – are trained by an organization called Nechi Institute on Alcoholism and Drug Education. These counsellors return to work on the reserves among their own people. Since the whole scheme is financed by the Alberta Drug and Alcohol Abuse Commission, a government body, there is a need to record progress not only for the satisfaction of the workers and the people themselves, but also to ensure continued funding. 'How,' ask the counsellors during their training, 'can we tell if we're getting anywhere?' And the answers are numerous: (a) records of contact-hours with alcoholics on the reserve; (b) records of the incidence of complaints of beatings of women and children by their menfolk, and of children by their parents; (c) records of school attendance by children, and of their atten-dance in a sober state (for the incidence of alcoholism is high among chil-dren); (d) records of drunken driving and other offences committed under the influence of alcohol.

This list indicates the need, in problems of this sort, to enlist the co-operation of other people in the community, such as the school teachers, police, and social workers.

The next step in the Glaser instructional model is the *design of the program*. The important thing here, for community development re-search, is that the program as agreed by the people and the agency should be so designed as to allow continuing assessment of change or lack of change. There should be opportunities for frequent data collection and feedback as part of the program itself. And this leads to the next element in Glaser's model, which is *monitoring and assessing*. In the instructional context to which the model applies it is proposed that there be carried out what are called formative evaluations, that is, periodic testing and evalu-ating the learner's progress during the program. This allows for revision and re-planning at stages during the process where it can be useful, rather than at the end of the process when it may well be too late to avoid damage. In community development this process and its methods should be one agreed to by the people in the community as part of the program, and the people should themselves again be involved in the data collecting, testing, and evaluating.

Finally, as this process takes place there will be valid and reliable grounds on which to adapt and to revise the total program, the final element in the cycle which begins at this point, with recasting of objectives. And at this point, if useful adaptation and revision takes place, the research will have taken place, such as is described in the model in chapter 2.

The action research model and the evaluation models drawn from education indicate that whereas community development shares with other humanistic endeavours a concern primarily for people and the development of their potential apart from the creation of material and physical things, and that whereas there is a justified reaction against kinds of social research which lean excessively on intellectualization and impersonality, there are nevertheless ways to avoid purely emotional, irrational, and unverifiable guess-work in this field. There are models and ways of disciplined thought and action which can be used in research for the purpose of making community development more effective in terms of its own goals. These can involve people in the community in the process both of development itself, and of the evaluation of such development.

To give a sharper and practical definition to what has been said, I attach, in appendix c, twenty rules of thumb for conducting an evaluation, prepared by Groteleuschen, Gooler, and Knox (1975). Though prepared in the context of adult education, and while tending to see the evaluation process primarily from the point of view of the 'program personnel,' with the people as 'clients,' the rules can be adapted to provide a good practical guide toward a more participatory process of evaluation in community development (Farmer and Papagiannis 1975).

GOALS AND OBJECTIVES – CONCLUSION

In the preface and chapter 2, I suggested that one of the propositions on which community development rests is that the process is seen in terms of ultimate goals. This might be taken as a 'motherhood' type of statement, but it seems worth risking the cynicism of those who may react in such a way, for the greater danger appears to lie in the opposite direction, namely, the abandonment of goals based on a value system, and the acceptance of less taxing objectives that can be neatly tied to some measureable activity or tangible object. And this danger is not illusory or conjectural. It has not been avoided in community development programs in the past, where the end is seen and accepted as being the completion of some physical asset, some set of behaviours, or a technology in the sense described in chapter 7, without regard for ultimate ends. Most definitions of community development, some of which are included in appendix b, fail to avoid the danger of expressing instrumentalities rather than goals.

Community development is a process, but it is a process towards some condition.

In the preface I suggested that community development rests on certain assumptions, which are: (a) that men are capable of perceiving and judging the conditions of their lives; (b) that they have the will and the capacity to plan together in accordance with these judgments to change that condition for the better; (c) that they can act together in accordance with these plans; (d) and that such a process can be seen in terms of certain values.

In one sense these 'certain values' are already implicit in the statement of these assumptions, in that they suggest a view of people as being active agents, capable of rational and beneficial actions for the attainment of collectively significant goals – what in chapter 5 I called a hypothesis about people. In other words, there is a certain set of values which relates to the nature of people as individuals; they are the values expressed in McGregor's theory y (1960).

Another set of values relates to the nature of communities of people, in the sense that we have been considering them in this book. In chapter 2, I referred to Deutsch's four dimensions of a group, or elements in its development. They are that the group possesses the quality of openness to information from the outside world; the quality of inner coherence, in that communication passes freely within the group; the capacity to learn and thereby to change; and the capacity to change its environment. These qualities can be said to express a value with regard to the community – a condition worthy of aspiring to. And in this sense the set of values becomes a set of objectives for the community.

The third set of values relates to the condition of the environment in which the community (and its members as individuals) exists. In chapter 2, I suggested that the very concept of community development implied a society which tolerates local groups which set out to formulate objectives involving changes in their conditions of living; it implies a hypothesis about government. And in chapter 5, I suggest that such a society was not simply and solely identical with western democracies such as Britain and the United States, where most thinking on community development originated. I suggested that in such countries as Tanzania and the People's Republic of China there existed social values which were hospitable to the idea and practice of community development. The social instrumentalities whereby the goodness of people was recognized and their development of ethical competence was allowed for, were not the preserve of one kind of democracy or country. In Goulet's terms, referred to in chapter 2, development ethics require freedom from servitude considered to be oppressive, and servitude comes in many forms.

In that same chapter, in the model based on Indian perceptions of their place in Canadian life, I suggested that there are other dimensions which have to be taken into account when we talk of social values: spirituality, consciousness, romanticism, the creation of and belief in symbols and myth, which cannot be dismissed.

These conclusions suggest, therefore, that with respect to community development, the practical business of political organization and objectives should reflect an awareness of wider human issues. It should prompt such questions as, 'In succeeding in our immediate objectives, what are our broader purposes and ultimate goals?'; What we are doing now (building a community hall, establishing a housing co-operative, counselling alcoholics, etc.) is a function of what?'

10

Summary

In the preface I indicate two principal themes of this book. The first is that in community development, as in all human activities, we carry out our actions not in an original emptiness of assumption and thought but according to some set of ideas which are conscious or not. These are generally called concepts, theories, or models. They are ways of organizing our perceptions of, and our actions in, the world around us. And in purposive activities like community development, when we do not start off with some model we generally seek out one or more which makes sense to us and which fits our personality, our situation, and our purposes. I say 'generally' because there are some people, whom we might call artists in action, who seem to be able to act intuitively in ways which achieve their purposes. Most of us depend on reconstructions of those actions, or reconstructions of experimental action from which theories have been formulated.

In the introduction (chapter 1) I go on to examine different kinds of models: analytical models, which help us to understand a current experience or an existing situation or structure, something like a snapshot; and process models, which help us to understand not just the relationship between elements in a structure but the dynamics of changing relationships, and the way things happen or can be made to happen, something like a moving picture. And I introduce the notion of paradigms, that is, broader mental sets, or world views, which influence the kinds of models we adopt. I suggest that when we are involved in social change we should be aware of the paradigm or paradigms within which we are living and acting, so as to increase the possibility of major and creative leaps in our conceptualization and action. And even within whatever paradigm it is that we acknowledge, the models which we choose to use are to be used not mechanically but creatively, adapted and moulded to our circumstances and needs.

Having suggested these possibilities, and some caution about the use of models, I propose, in part one, a concept of community and a model of community development as a process. The concept of community relates not to geography and location but to the shared interests and common objectives of groups of people, who may or may not be situated in a definable locality but who are in communication with one another. The model of community development encompasses two perspectives: development seen as both a learning and a political process. It is a learning process in that it assumes that people have the capacity to perceive and judge the condition of their lives, and to adopt behaviours to improve that condition. It assumes, moreover, that in the course of this learning they can look critically at the reigning paradigms of the society in which they live. It is a political process because it seeks collective goals through the marshalling of the energies and resources of the community.

Part two takes the main stages of the proposed model of community development – i.e., learning of our existing situation; formulating objectives for a change in that situation; learning group skills in planning and organization, group decision-making and action; and evaluation – and applies some models which appear to be appropriate to those stages. Some of these models are analytical in the sense that they help us to sort out the elements in the situation, such as those in chapter 5 where we consider factors of environment and culture, and in chapter 7 where we consider the elements in a socio-technical system. The models of learning in chapter 4 are partly process models in that they help us understand what goes on in the process of learning, and partly analytical in that they draw attention to underlying views of human nature which form the basic elements in the two main theoretical approaches. In other words, these models, and the others, do not give specific answers; they are ways of helping us arrive at answers for ourselves.

The remaining models, relating to group processes, organization development, decision-making, and evaluation, are process models in that they suggest ways of organizing our actions at various stages of the community development process. In other words, the process models suggest a number of techniques which can be adopted within the general outlines of the model – such as T-groups, the use of instruments like the one shown in appendix B, group data collecting, brainstorming, force-field analysis, and action research.

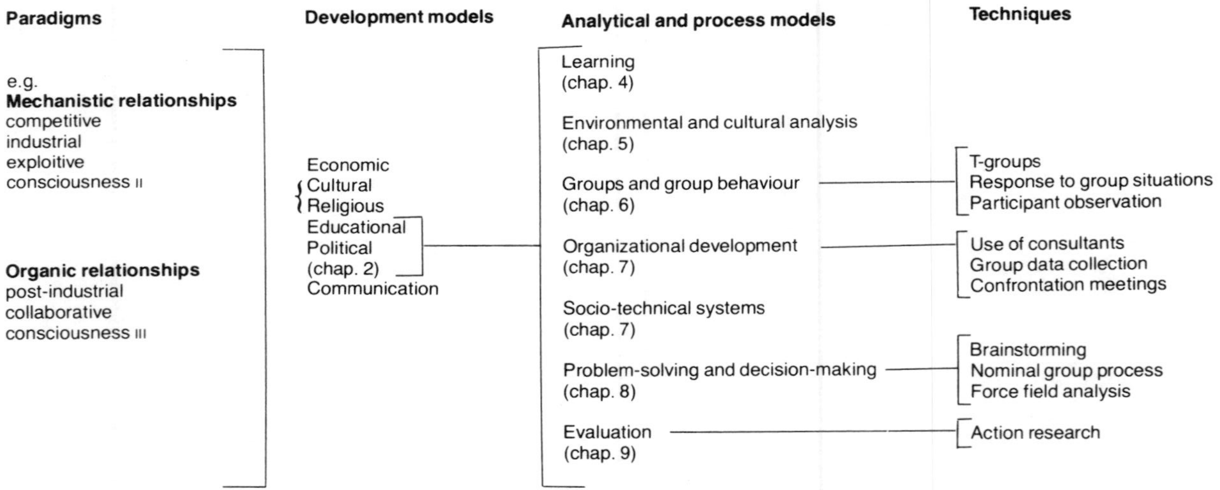

Paradigms

e.g.
Mechanistic relationships
competitive
industrial
exploitive
consciousness II

Organic relationships
post-industrial
collaborative
consciousness III

Development models

Economic
Cultural
Religious
Educational
Political
(chap. 2)
Communication

Analytical and process models

Learning
(chap. 4)

Environmental and cultural analysis
(chap. 5)

Groups and group behaviour
(chap. 6)

Organizational development
(chap. 7)

Socio-technical systems
(chap. 7)

Problem-solving and decision-making
(chap. 8)

Evaluation
(chap. 9)

Techniques

T-groups
Response to group situations
Participant observation

Use of consultants
Group data collection
Confrontation meetings

Brainstorming
Nominal group process
Force field analysis

Action research

FIGURE 12   Paradigms, models, and techniques

The discussion as it is summarized above can be represented diagrammatically (Figure 12) to indicate the relationship between paradigms, models, and techniques as the terms have been used in the book. In particular, the techniques referred to are shown in relation to the analytical and process models discussed in the various chapters in part two. With regard to paradigms, no particular one has been assumed in the course of the argument. On the other hand, it has revealed a posture which is critical to the dominant contemporary paradigm of mechanistic relations and points toward the alternative of organic, collaborative relationships.

The question of the scope of community development has been inherent in all this. In chapter 2, I suggested that in the mass society, the industrial society, community development is marginal to the main process of social and political change. Jackson (1973) has made this argument with particular reference to Britain, and he suggests that claims made on behalf of community development in such conditions are less than completely honest. Certainly, there seem to be enough ambiguities in the various definitions of community development to have caused many of those concerned with it to claim too much for it or to have failed to set realistic limits to it. On the other hand, it was pointed out that there are increasing indications, through writers like Trist, Curle, Musgrove, Reich, and Roszak, that the emerging post-industrial society looks more hospitable to the philosophy and practice represented by community development.

But even without that, the process of community development as discussed in this book deserves notice. I have suggested a definition of community as a group of persons who, having become aware of a problem – through the tensions caused by it – learn about its circumstances and then form a commonly agreed objective to overcome it. The development of the community is achieved through action toward those objectives. The model of the community development process put forward in chapter 2 suggests that it then proceeds in cycles: achieving this objective, realizing new tensions, further learning, forming new objectives, devising new courses of action, evaluating that action, and so on. What is involved is a hierarchy of objectives, each formed and achieved within a certain environment as described in the discussion of social systems in chapter 3 and socio-technical systems in chapter 7. Systems theory suggests environmental restraints which will affect the achievement of each objective, some of these being the social and political philosophy and social structure within which the community exists (chapter 5). But it also suggests that each system and subsystem is not merely passive but can have an effect on its environment and the larger system of which it is a part. Where the problem is one which extends beyond local limits, and the community is one which extends beyond a fairly clearly delineated geographical location, the objectives will extend beyond that limit. In any case, whatever the community, its doings will likely have a wider effect.

What characterizes community development in terms of social action is that it places between the individual on the one hand and the continuing units of the state on the other, intervening functional communities which engage people in learning and in action to achieve objectives formulated by them. Friedmann (1973,196-7) uses the term 'task-oriented work groups' to denote groups similar to what are defined in this discussion as communities. He suggests that they can come together in a cellular structure of clustered networks to influence political affairs. In chapter 2, I referred to the emergence of coalitions of communities in the United States.

Community development is marginal in three respects, one in the manner in which some of it has been carried out, and the others inherent in its nature. The first arises from the woolly, if well-meaning, intentions, and lack of vigorous application to clearly perceived objectives, that characterizes some work in this field. The other two are more important. First, the objectives and action of community development are not a part of the formal representative and executive mechanisms of government in which a state's political directions are determined. But second – and here is a paradox – the basic philosophy of self-direction and direct citizen participation which is inherent in community development, at the intervening community level, can be and often are, seen by people in the formal government institutions as being subversive of the control mechanisms which they manage, so that in many cases community development is *made* to be marginal by such people. It is sometimes even suppressed. So in this paradoxical way community development is *not* marginal. Effective action at the level of community subsystems can influence other subsystems in the wider political and social systems, and people in community development can acquire knowledge, attitudes, and skills which can be carried over into participation in a more formal government of the wider system; in other words, community development is an educational process which, once begun, is difficult to contain.

There is a small community in northern Alberta called Wabasca, where some years ago a community development field worker was stationed as part of the development program which came under the Human Resources Development Authority. I have referred in chapter 4 to the way in which this provincial program was phased out by the government, largely because of the concern of political leaders and senior administrators about the repercussions of getting people too involved in these ways. The people of that community staged a march to the capital, Edmonton, to press for more development in their area. But now, after almost ten years, what those people learned about organization and the marshalling of information is being put to good use. The brief and presentations made by the community's leaders to government are impressing bureaucrats with their sophistication and good sense, and the area is again showing signs of advance, not only in such economic enterprises as sawmills and oil sands exploration, but in the involvement of the local people in general development.

And that goes not only for community development and contact between groups, but also for contact between persons. We teach what we are; I teach what I am.

APPENDICES

A

Some definitions of
community development

The term 'community development' has come into international usage to connote the processes by which the *efforts of the people themselves are united with those of governmental authorities to improve the economic, social and cultural conditions of communities*, to integrate these communities into the life of the nation, and to enable them to contribute fully to national progress.

This complex of processes is then made up of two essential elements: the *participation of the people* themselves in efforts to improve their level of living with as much reliance as possible on their own initiative, and the provision of *technical and other services* in ways which encourage initiative, self-help, and mutual help and make them more effective. It is expressed in programs designed to achieve a wide variety of specific improvements. (See Du Sautoy 1964,121.)

B. BRITAIN

(a) Community development is a movement designed to promote *better living for the whole community with the active participation and, if possible, on the initiative of the community*, but if this initiative is not forthcoming spontaneously, by the use of techniques for arousing and stimulating it in order to secure the active and enthusiastic response of the movement. (See HMSO 1954.)

(b) Community development is only a part of the over-all process of the development of communities. It is the part of the process which can be distinguished by the following ingredients: (a) self-help; (b) attention paid to the people's *'felt needs;'* (c) attention paid to the social, traditional, and other aspects of the *community* as a whole. It usually operates in four main fields: (a) adult literacy and basic social education; (b) specialized work among women and youth; (c) self-help construction projects; (d) extension education in various 'nation building' fields. It may also concern itself with co-operatives and the stimulation of cottage industry. (See Du Sautoy 1964,125-6.)

C. UNITED STATES

(a) Community development is a continuous, or intermittent, process of social action by which the *people of a community organize themselves* informally or formally for democratic planning and action; *define their common and group 'felt needs'* and problems; *make group and individual plans* to meet their felt needs and solve their problems; *execute these plans* with a maximum of reliance upon resources found within the community; and *supplement community resources* when necessary with services and the material assistance from governmental or private agencies outside the community. (See Green 1963; this definition is a slight modification by Dr Green of a definition used by the US International Co-operation Administration and quoted in Du Sautoy 1964.)

(b) (i) A social process by which human beings can become more competent to live with and gain some *control over local aspects* of a frustrating and changing world.

(ii) A progression of events that is planned by the participants to serve goals they progressively chose. The events point to changes in a group and in individuals that can be termed growth in social sensitivity and competence. (See Biddle and Biddle 1965, 78-9.)

(c) Organized efforts of people to improve the condition of *community life* and the capacity of the people for *participation, self-direction, and integrated effort in community* affairs. (See Dunham 1970,140.)

(d) The key word is process ... a change in an attitude of mind, whether personal or collective, that results in a change of behavior and the pursuit of a course of action hitherto rejected or not understood. We avoid associating community development with any particular program, be the setting rural or urban' (Brokensha and Hodge 1969,47.)

D. CANADA

(a) Community development is an *educational-motivation process* designed to create conditions favourable to economic and social change, if possible on the initiative of *the community*, but if this initiative is not forthcoming spontaneously, then techniques for arousing and stimulating it in order to secure the fullest participation of the community must be utilized. (See Special Planning Secretariat 1965,2.)

(b) The process of facilitation *in solving problems* as identified by the community itself. (See A. Stinson in Draper 1971,262.)

(c) *Community development in Canada has still to define its area for action, as well as the issues it should tackle.* It can not simply be concerned with development-as-increase in resources or productivity (as it primarily is in emerging countries) but also and foremost with *two closely linked problem areas: the allocation of assets within our society, and the allocation of power.* (See F.J. Bregha in Draper 1971,73-5.)

E. INDIA

(a) A method and an ideology for promoting the development of *rural areas of the country on democratic lines and with the active participation of the people.* (See Mukerji 1967,26.)

(b) A method by which all the technical services of government can be channelled down to meet and assist the gigantic developing potential power of hundred and thousands of effectively *organized village groups.* (See B. Mukerji quoted in Taylor 1956.)

F. RHODESIA

Community development may be summed up, *insofar as central government's role is concerned,* as an active, planned, and organized effort to place *responsibility for decision-making in local affairs on the freely chosen representatives of responsible people at the community and local government levels,* and to assist people to acquire the attitudes, knowledge, skills, and resources required to solve, through communal self-help and organization, as wide a range of *local* problems as possible in their own order of priority. (See Government of Rhodesia 1965.)

B

Reactions to group situations

You will be presented with one-sentence descriptions of a lot of incidents of the kind that frequently occur in classrooms or groups.

Each of these descriptions is given in an incomplete sentence that can be finished in either of two ways, A or B. Decide which way you prefer to finish each sentence. On the separate response sheet mark either A or B (not both) opposite the number of the sentence, depending on which of the two ways you would end that sentence.

Make your selections quickly. Don't linger over the items – your first impression is good enough. Please do not leave any items.

1 When I wanted to work with Frank, I ...
   A felt we could do well together
   B asked if it would be all right with him

2 When the group wanted his views about the task, Sam ...
   A wondered why they wanted his views
   B thought of what he might tell them

3 When the leader made no comment, I ...
   A offered a suggestion of what to do
   B wondered what to do next

4 When Don said he felt closest to me, I ...
   A was glad
   B was suspicious

5 When I felt helpless, I ...
  A wished that the leader would help me
  B found a friend to tell how I felt

6 When Henry was annoyed, Ray ...
  A thought of a way to explain the situation to him
  B realized just how he felt

7 When Ned felt eager to go to work, he ...
  A got mad at the late-comers
  B wanted to team up with Jim

8 When Glenn bawled me out, I ...
  A lost interest in what we were supposed to be doing
  B thought that some of his ideas would be useful

9 When the leader lost interest, Mort ...
  A suggested a way to get everybody working
  B started talking with his neighbours

10 When Phil felt warm and friendly, he ...
  A accomplished a lot more
  B liked just about everyone

11 When the leader was unsure of himself, Norm ...
  A wanted to leave the group
  B didn't know what to do

12 When the group just couldn't seem to get ahead, I ...
  A felt like dozing off
  B became annoyed with them

13 When the group wasn't interested, I ...
  A just didn't feel like working
  B thought that the leader should do something about it

14 When the leader said he felt the same way I did, I ...
  A was glad that I had his approval
  B thought we would probably begin to make progress now

15 When I became angry at Jack, I ...
A felt like dozing off
B ridiculed his comments

16 When the leader wanted me to tell the class about my plan, I ...
A wished I could get out of it
B wished that he would introduce it for me

17 When Art criticized Bert, I ...
A wished that the teacher would help Bert
B felt grateful to Art for really expressing what we both felt

18 When Henry and Mary enjoyed each other's company so much, I ...
A thought that I'd like to leave the room
B felt angry

19 When the leader changed the subject, Al ...
A suggested that they stick to the original topic
B felt glad that the leader was finally taking over

20 When the others became so keen on really working hard, I ...
A made an effort to make really good suggestions
B felt much more warmly toward them

21 When I felt angry enough to boil, I ...
A wanted to throw something
B wished that the leader would do something about it

22 When Lee was not paying attention, I ...
A did not know what to do
B wanted to tell him he was wasting our time

23 When Harry thought that he needed a lot of help, Martin ...
A warmly encouraged him to get it
B helped him analyze the problem

24 When Jack reported his results so far, I ...
A laughed at him
B was bored

25 When everyone felt angry, I ...
A suggested that they stop and evaluate the situation
B was glad that the leader stepped in

26 When no one was sticking to the point, I ...
A got bored with the whole thing
B called for clarification of the topic

27 When Herb said he felt especially friendly toward me, I ...
A wanted to escape
B wanted to ask his advice

28 When the group agreed that it needed more information about how members felt, I ...
A described my feelings to the group
B wasn't sure I wanted to discuss my feelings

29 When the leader offered to help Carl, Joe ...
A wanted help too
B resented the leader's offer

30 When Dave and Lou argued, I ...
A asked Hank how he felt about them
B felt like telling them to stop obstructing

31 When Chuck felt especially close to Steve, he ...
A let him know it
B hoped Steve could turn to him for assistance

32 When several members dropped out of the discussion, Henry ...
A thought it was time to find out where the group was going
B got sore at what he thought was their discourtesy

33 When Stan told me he felt uncertain about what should be done, I ...
A suggested that he wait awhile before making any decisions
B suggested that he get more information

34 When Jim realized that quite a few people were taking digs at each other, he ...

    A wanted to call the group to order
    B got angry at the stupidity of their behaviour

35 When the group suggested a procedure, I ...
    A thought the teacher ought to express his approval or disapproval of it
    B thought we ought to decide whether to carry it out

36 When Ed seemed to be daydreaming, Bill ...
    A winked at Joe
    B felt freer to doodle

37 When Tom and Mary arrived twenty minutes late for the meeting, the group ...
    A went right on working
    B was very annoyed

38 During the argument, Roy's opposition caused Earl to ...
    A withdraw from the discussion
    B look to the teacher for support

39 When Marvin suggested we evaluate how well we were working as a group, I ...
    A was glad that the period was almost over
    B gladly backed him up

40 When the group seemed to be losing interest, Pat ...
    A became angry with the other members
    B thought it might just as well adjourn

41 Together John and Fred ...
    A wasted the group's time
    B supported one another's arguments

42 When Hal offered to help me, I ...
    A said I was sorry, but I had something else to do
    B was pleased that we would be partners

43 When the other group became so interested in their work, George ...
    A wanted to ask their leader if he could join them
    B felt resentful that his group was so dull

44 When Art left the meeting early, Dick ...
  A and Michael told each other what they felt about Art
  B was glad that he had gone

45 When Lou turned to me, I ...
  A wished that he would mind his own business
  B asked him for help

46 When Hal felt hostile to the group, he ...
  A wished he had not come to the meeting ...
  B was glad that Bob felt the same way

47 While Dan was helping me, I ...
  A became annoyed with his superior attitude
  B felt good about being with him

48 When I lost track of what Paul was saying I ...
  A asked the teacher to explain Paul's idea to me
  B was pleased that it was Mike who explained Paul's idea to me

49 While the group was expressing friendly feelings toward Bill, Ken ...
  A thought that now Bill would be able to work
  B opened a book and started to read

50 When the leader offered to help him, Pete ...
  A said that he did not want any help
  B realized that he did need help from someone

See Table A.1 for scoring and Figure A.1 for tally sheet.

METHOD OF MARKING TALLY SHEET – EXAMPLES

Say that for statement 1 the respondent marked alternative A rather than B, showing a preference for pairing over dependency. A mark for this answer would be placed in square 2.5.

Say that for statement 2 the respondent marked alternative B rather than A, showing a preference for work over fight. A mark for this answer would be placed in square 1.3.

Say that for statement 11 the respondent marked alternative B rather than A, showing a preference for dependency over flight. A mark for this answer would be placed in square 5.4.

TABLE A.1
Scoring key for reactions to group situations

1	A–P		18	A–FL		35	A–D
	B–D			B–F			B–W
2	A–F		19	A–W		36	A–P
	B–W			B–D			B–FL
3	A–W		20	A–W		37	A–W
	B–D			B–P			B–F
4	A–P		21	A–F		38	A–FL
	B–F			B–D			B–D
5	A–D		22	A–D		39	A–FL
	B–P			B–F			B–P
6	A–W		23	A–P		40	A–F
	B–P			B–W			B–FL
7	A–F		24	A–F		41	A–FL
	B–P			B–FL			B–P
8	A–FL		25	A–W		42	A–FL
	B–W			B–D			B–P
9	A–W		26	A–FL		43	A–D
	B–P			B–W			B–F
10	A–W		27	A–FL		44	A–P
	B–P			B–D			B–F
11	A–FL		28	A–W		45	A–F
	B–D			B–FL			B–D
12	A–FL		29	A–D		46	A–FL
	B–F			B–F			B–P
13	A–FL		30	A–P		47	A–F
	B–D			B–F			B–P
14	A–D		31	A–P		48	A–D
	B–W			B–D			B–P
15	A–FL		32	A–W		49	A–W
	B–F			B–F			B–FL
16	A–FL		33	A–FL		50	A–F
	B–D			B–W			B–W
17	A–D		34	A–W			
	B–P			B–F			

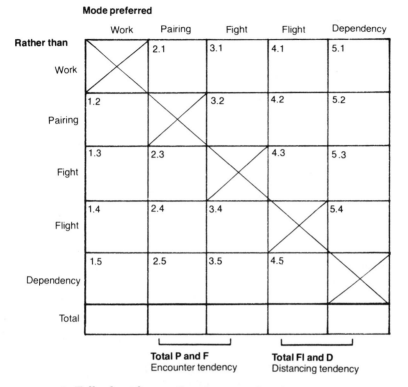

FIGURE A.1 Tally sheet for reactions to group situations

On the other hand, if for statement 11 the respondent marked alternative A rather than B, showing a preference for flight over dependency, a mark for this answer would be placed in square 4.5.

In other words, one selects the vertical column under the heading indicated as being preferred in that response, and places a mark in that column, in the square level with the heading rejected in that response. The totals for 'pairing' and 'fight' together show a general tendency to want to encounter situations and people, while the totals for 'flight' and 'dependency' together show a general tendency to be diffident toward situations and people. As a group exercise the totals for each group member under the five columns can be aggregated to show a group profile.

C

Twenty rules of thumb
for conducting an evaluation

These rules of thumb are taken from Groteleuschen, Gooler, and Knox in Farmer and Papagiannis (1975). The procedures used in actually conducting an evaluation are determined in part by what questions are being addressed by the evaluation, the techniques selected for collecting data, and the audiences to whom the data will be reported. Most evaluations are unique to the situation being evaluated. There are, however, some general rules of thumb which might be attended to in successfully conducting an evaluation.

1 Someone needs to be responsible for conducting the evaluation. Too often, all the details involved in conducting an evaluation are allowed to fall through the cracks because no one has been designated to worry about details. Most evaluation plans are not automatically implemented without someone taking charge.

2 Make sure everyone is formed about what is going on in an evaluation activity. Evaluation ought not to be a mysterious, cloak and dagger operation. Go over evaluation plans, including data processing plans, with all relevant program personnel, so there are no surprises with respect to what is going to happen in the evaluation.

3 Insofar as possible, be redundant in data gathering on the concerns that are important to the evaluation. Seek to ask about a program (or its aspects) in several different ways. Insight and understanding often comes with repeated encounter.

4 Give careful direction for all data gathering instruments. Make sure the person from whom you are requesting information understands what you are asking for.

5 Be aware of the pressures and constraints on the program being evaluated. If people are being harassed on a day you are asking them for information, be prepared to come back another time. Do not intrude into the program.

6 Do not promise things which you cannot deliver. This is especially true with respect to time, promises of anonymity, and keeping of confidences.

7 Be aware that you are investigating aspects that are of personal and professional importance to the people working in a program. Do not dismiss a person's work without giving it careful attention.

8 Insofar as possible, be unobtrusive.

9 Early on, establish ground rules about who will have access to evaluation results, and when.

10 Collect only those data for which you have some rationale.

11 Keep your eyes open for the unexpected or unintended. Do not let an evaluation plan act as a blinder.

12 In most cases, evaluators ought not to assume the role of decision-maker. Evaluators might spell out options, but ought not to allow themselves to make decisions for the program administrator or teacher.

13 Be open and responsive to client needs and interests. Remember that client interests may shift as the evaluation progresses.

14 Be positive. Being an evaluator does not mean you look only for the negative ... Assume a project is basically good, and that evaluation is an attempt to make it better.

15 Provide feedback as appropriate. Be flexible, but not premature, in sharing evaluative data.

16 Before you ask questions, make sure you understand what some of the consequences of asking those questions might be. Make sure you are willing to deal with those consequences.

17 Be businesslike. Show people you know what you are doing without being apologetic or pompous.

18 Be able to tolerate ambiguity. You may not always get answers to the questions you ask.

19 If possible, get someone to react to your evaluation plans before implementing the plans. But know when to stop asking for advice.

20 Give a personal thanks to those who participated in the evaluation, insofar as possible. People have given up some part of their time to assist in the evaluation.

Bibliography

Ahmed, Monzoor and Philip H. Coombs, eds. (1975) *Education for Rural Development: Case Studies for Planners*. New York: Praeger

Alberta Commission on Educational Planning (1972) *A Choice of Futures*. Edmonton: Queen's Printer

Alinsky, S. (1972) *Rules for Radicals*. New York: Vintage Books

Allport, G. (1955) *Becoming*. New Haven: Yale University Press

Anderson, C.A. (1961-2) 'Methodology of comparative education.' *International Review of Education* 7

Angyal, A. (1969) 'A logic of systems.' In F.E. Emery, ed. *Systems Thinking*. Harmondsworth: Penguin

Argyris, C. (1962) *Interpersonal Competence and Organizational Effectiveness*. Homewood, Ill: Irwin

Arrighi, G.L. (1966) 'The political economy of Rhodesia.' *New Left Review* (London) no. 39

Bales, R.F. (1950) *Interaction Process Analysis*. Cambridge, Mass: Addison-Wesley

Bandura, A. and R.H. Walters (1963) *Social Learning and Personality Development*. New York: Holt, Rinehart and Winston

Beckhard, R. (1969) *Organization Development: Strategies and Models*. Reading, Mass: Addison-Wesley

Bell, D. (1966) 'The adequacy of our concepts.' In B. Gross, ed. *A Great Society?* New York: Basic Books

Benne, K. and P. Sheats (1961) 'Functional roles of group members.' In Bradford, Leland P., ed. *Group Development*. Washington: NTL

Bennis, W. (1969) *Organization Development: Its Nature, Origins and Prospects*. Reading, Mass: Addison-Wesley

– and H. Shepard (1956) 'A theory of group development.' Human Relations 9

– and P.E. Slater (1969) *The Temporary Society*. New York: Harper Colophon

Bernthal, W.F. (1968) 'Value perspectives in management decision.' In M.S. Wadia, ed. *Management and the Behavioral Sciences*. Boston: Allyn and Bacon.

Biddle, W.W. and L.J. (1966) *The Community Development Process*. New York: Holt, Rinehart and Winston

Bion, W. (1961) *Experience in Groups*. New York: Basic Books

Bloom, B.S. *et al.* (1956) *Taxonomy of Educational Objectives, Handbook I – Cognitive Domain*. New York: McKay

– (1964) *Taxonomy of Educational Objectives, Handbook II – Affective Domain*. New York: McKay

Brokensha, D. (1974) 'Maximum feasible participation, USA.' *Community Development Journal* 9, no. 1

– and P. Hodge (1969) *Community Development: An Interpretation*. San Francisco: Chandler

Brookover, W.B. and D. Gottlieb (1964) *A Sociology of Education*. New York: American Book Co

Buckley, W. (1967) *Sociology and Modern Systems Theory*. Englewood Cliffs, NJ: Prentice Hall

Cadwallader, M.L. (1969) 'The cybernetics of analysis of change in complex social organizations.' In J.A. Litterer, *Organizations*, vol. 2. New York: Wiley

Camaro, Dom Helder (1975) Interview with Jacques Babin. Co-operation Canada, May-June. Ottawa: Canadian International Development Agency

Carkhuff, R.R. and B.C. Berenson (1967) *Beyond Counselling and Therapy*. New York: Holt, Rinehart and Winston

Central African Examiner (1973) Salisbury, Rhodesia: Aug. and Sept.

Chin, R. (1964) 'The utility of systems models and development models for practitioners.' In W. Bennis, K. Benne, and R. Chin, eds. *The Planning of Change*. New York: Holt, Rinehart and Winston

– and K. Benne (1969) 'General strategies for affecting change in human systems.' In W. Bennis, K. Benne, and R. Chin, eds. *The Planning of Change*, 2nd ed. New York: Holt, Rinehart and Winston

Cicourel, A.V. and J.L. Kitsuse (1963) *The Educational Decision-Makers*. New York: Bobbs Merrill

Clutton-Brock, G. and M. (1972) *Cold Comfort Confronted*. London: Mowbray

Cohen, K.J. and A.M. Cyert (1965) *Theory of the Firm*. Englewood Cliffs, NJ: Prentice Hall

Combs, A.W. and D. Snygg (1959) *Individual Behavior*. New York: Harper and Row

Coombs, Philip H., Roy C. Prosser, and Monzoor Ahmed (1973) *New Paths to Learning for Rural Children and Youth*. International Council for Educational Development

Crone, C.D. (1977) 'Autopsy or checkup?' *World Education Reports* no. 1r, Oct.

Crowfoot, J.E. and M.A. Chesler (1974) 'Contemporary perspectives on planned change: a comparison.' *Journal of Applied Behavioral Science* 10, no. 3

Curle, A. (1972) *Mystics and Militants*. London: Tavistock

Davis, K. (1971) 'Can business afford to ignore social responsibilities?' In W.T. Greenwood, ed. *Issues in Business and Society*. Boston: Houghton, Mifflin

Delbecq, A.L. and A.H. Van Den Ven (1971) 'A group process model for problem identification and program planning.' *Journal of Applied Behavioral Science* 7, no. 4

Derbyshire, R.L. (1966) 'The sociology of exclusion: implications for teaching adults.' *Adult Education* (Washington) 7, no. 1

Deutsch, K.W. (1952) 'On communication models in the social sciences.' *Public Opinion Quarterly* 16

Development Associates (1975) Documentation and analysis of development programs in Canada. Unpublished report for Department of Regional Economic Expansion, Ottawa

Draper, J., ed. (1971) *Citizen Participation: Canada*. Toronto: New Press

Dunham, A. (1970) *The New Community Organization*. New York: Crowell

Du Sautoy, P. (1964) *The Organization of a Community Development Programme*. London: Oxford University Press

Edmonton Journal (1976) April 20

Ellul, J. (1964) *The Technological Society*. New York: Alfred A. Knopf

Emery, F.E. and E.L. Trist (1969) 'Socio-technical systems.' In F.E. Emery, ed. *Systems Thinking*. Harmondsworth: Penguin

Erasmus, C.J. (1968) 'Community development and the encogido syndrome.' *Human Organization* 27, no. 1

Etzioni, A. (1964) *Modern Organizations*. Englewood Cliffs, NJ: Prentice Hall

– (1968) *The Active Society*. London: Collier-Macmillan

Farmer, J.A. and G. Papagiannis (1975) *Program Evaluation: Functional Education for Family Life Planning*, III. New York: World Education

Festinger, L. (1957) *A Theory of Cognitive Dissonance*. Palo Alto: Stanford University Press

Findhorn Foundation University of Light (1975) Guest Programme. Forres, Scotland: Findhorn Foundation

Freire, P. (1970) 'Cultural action and conscientization.' Harvard Educational Review no. 40

– (1972) *Pedagogy of the Oppressed*. New York: Herder and Herder

French, J.R.P. and B.H. Raven (1959) 'The bases of social power.' In D. Cartwright, ed. *Studies in Social Power*. Ann Arbor: University of Michigan Press

Friedmann, J. (1973) *Retracking America: A Theory of Transactive Planning*. New York: Anchor/Doubleday

Gagne, R.M. (1967) *The Conditions of Learning*. New York: Holt, Rinehart and Winston

Giorgi, A. (1975) 'Humanistic psychology and metapsychology.' Unpublished paper presented at the Fourth Centre Conference on Theoretical Psychology. Edmonton, University of Alberta

Glaser, R. (1965) 'Toward a behavioral science base for instructional design.' In R. Glaser, ed. *Teaching Machines and Programmed Learning*, II. Washington: NEA

Goulet, D. (1971) *The Cruel Choice*. New York: Atheneum

Government of Rhodesia (1965) *Local Government and Community Development*. Salisbury: Government Printer, CSR 44-1965

Green, J.W. (1963) *Community Development*. University of Rhodesia: Institute of Adult Education

Groombridge, B. (1972) *Television and the People*. Harmondsworth: Penguin

Hagan, E.E. (1964) *On the Theory of Social Change*. London; Tavistock Publications

Haiman, F.S. (1951) *Group Leadership and Democratic Action*. Boston: Houghton Mifflin

Hall, Budd (1975) 'Participatory research: an approach for change.' *Convergence* 8, no. 2

Hall, J.T. and R.A. Dixon (1974) 'Cybernetic sessions: a technique for gathering ideas.' *Annual Handbook for Group Facilitators*. University Associates Publishers Inc

Hampton-Turner, C. (1970) *Radical Man*. Cambridge, Mass: Schenkman

Harrison, J.F.C. (1961) *Learning and Living, 1960-1970*. Toronto: University of Toronto Press

Henaut, D.T. (1971-2) 'Powerful catalyst.' *Challenge for Change*. National Film Board of Canada no. 7, winter

Hilgard, E.R. and G.H. Bower (1966) *Theories of Learning*, 3rd ed. New York: Appleton-Century-Crofts

Hill, M.J. and R.M. Issacharoff (1971) *Community Action and Race Relations*. London: Oxford University Press

Hill, W.F. (1963) *Learning*. San Francisco: Chandler

Hillery, G. (1955) 'Definitions of community areas of agreement.' *Rural Sociology* 20

Hinton, W. (1968) *Fanshen*. New York: Vintage

HMSO (1954) Report of the *Ashbridge Conference on Social Development*. Colonial Office Miscellaneous no. 523

Homans, G.C. (1950) *The Human Group*. New York: Harcourt, Brace and World

Husen, T. (1974) *The Learning Society*. London: Methuen

Illich, I. (1970) *Deschooling Society*. New York: Harper and Row

Jackson, K. (1973) 'The marginality of community development.' *International Review of Community Development* nos. 29/30

Jenkins, D.H. (1964) 'Force field analysis applied to a school situation.' In W. Bennis, K. Benne, and R. Chin, eds. *The Planning of Change*, 1st ed. New York: Holt, Rinehart and Winston

Johnson, W.W. (1974) *The Search for Transcendence*. New York: Harper Colophon

Journal of Humanistic Psychology (1971) Editorial 11, no. 2

Jung, C.G. (1923) *Psychological Types*. London: Routledge and Kegan Paul

– (1972) Commentary to R. Wilhelm, *The Secret of the Golden Flower*. London: Routledge and Kegan Paul

Kaplan, A. (1964) *The Conduct of Inquiry*. San Francisco: Chandler

Karch, A.V. (1971-2) 'VTR in Drumheller, Alberta.' *Challenge for Change*, National Film Board of Canada no. 7, winter

Katz, D. and R.L. Kahn (1966) *The Social Psychology of Organizations*. New York: Wiley

Kelley, H.H. and J.W. Thibaut (1968) 'Group problem-solving.' In G. Lindzey and E. Aronson, eds. *The Handbook of Social Psychology* 2nd ed., vol. 4. Cambridge, Mass: Addison-Wesley

Kelly, T. (1970) *A History of Adult Education in Great Britain*. Liverpool University Press

Kuhn, T.S. (1970) 'The structure of scientific revolutions.' In D. Neurath, R. Carnap, and C. Morris, eds. *Foundations of the Unity of Science*, 2nd ed., vol. 2. Chicago: University of Chicago Press

Lawrence, P.R. and J.W. Lorch (1969) 'Differentiation and integration in complex organizations.' In J.A. Litterer, ed. *Organizations*, vol. 2. New York: Wiley

Lewin, K. (1947) 'Frontiers in group dynamics.' *Human Relations* 1, no. 1

– (1948) *Resolving Social Conflicts*. New York: Harper and Row

– (1965) 'Group decisions and social change.' In H. Proshansky and B. Seidenberg, eds. *Basic Studies in Social Psychology*. New York: Holt, Rinehart and Winston

Lindgren, H.C. (1967) 'Theories of human learning revisited.' In E.M. Bower and W.G. Hollister, eds. *Behavioral Science Frontiers in Education*. New York: Wiley

Locke, J. (1894) *Essay Concerning Human Understanding, Book IV* (ed. A.C. Fraser), vol. 2, chap. 17, section 14. Oxford: Clarendon Press

– (1963) *Some Thoughts Concerning Education. Works*, new ed. 1823. vol. IX. Reprint by Scientia Verlag Aalen, Germany.

Loomis, C.P. (1960) *Social Systems*. Princeton: Van Nostrand

Lovatt, T. (1975) *Adult Education, Community Development and the Working Class*. London: Ward Lock Educational

Lowe, John (1970) *Adult Education and Nation Building*. Edinburgh: Edinburgh University Press

Luft, J. (1970) *Group Processes*. Palo Alto: National Press Books

Lumsdaine, A.A. (1965) 'Assessing the effectiveness of institutional programs.' In R. Glaser, ed. *Teaching Machines and Programmed Learning, II*. Washington: NEA

Malinowski, B. (1944) *A Scientific Theory of Culture*. Chapel Hill: University of N. Carolina Press

Mandelbaum, J. (1972) *Community and Communications*. New York: Norton

Mannheim, K. (1936) *Ideology and Utopia*. New York: Harcourt, Brace Harvest Books

Mao Tse-Tung (1972) *Quotations from Chairman Mao Tse-Tung*. Peking: Foreign Language Press

March, J.G. and H.A. Simon (1958) *Organizations*. New York: Wiley

Marris, P. and M. Rein, (1967) *Dilemmas of Social Reform*. New York: Atherton Press

Maslow, A.H. (1968) *Toward a Psychology of Being*. New York: Van Nostrand Reinhold

Matson, F.W. (1973) *Without/Within: Behaviourism and Humanism*. Monterey: Brooks/Cole

May, E. (1960) *The Human Problems of an Industrial Civilization*. New York: Viking Press

May, Rollo (1971) *Newsletter of the Association on Humanistic Psychology 8*, no. 4

McClelland, D. (1961) *The Achieving Society*. Princeton, NJ: Van Nostrand

McGregor, D. (1960) *The Human Side of Enterprise*. New York: McGraw-Hill

McIver, R.M. (1924) *Community*. London: Macmillan

McLeish, J. (1969) *The Theory of Social Change*. London: Routledge and Kegan Paul

Mead, G.M. (1934) *Mind, Self and Society*. Chicago: University of Chicago Press

Meier, R.L. (1962) *A Communications Theory of Urban Growth*. Cambridge: MIT Press.

Mezirow, J.D. (1963) *Dynamics of Community Development*. New York: Scarecrow Press

Mial, D. and H.C., eds. (1961) *Forces in Community Development*. Washington: NTL and NEA

Millar, N.E. and J. Dollard (1964) *Social Learning and Imitation*. New Haven: Yale University Press

Miller, H.L. (1964) *Teaching and Learning in Adult Education*. New York: Macmillan

Mogar, R.E. (1969) 'Toward a psychological theory of education.' *Journal of Humanistic Psychology* 9, no. 1

Moore, W.E. (1963) *Social Change*. Englewood Cliffs, NJ: Prentice Hall

Moravia, A. (1969) *The Red Book and the Great Wall*. London: Panther

Mukerji, B. (1967) *Community Development in India*. Bombay: Orient Longmans

Musgrove, F. (1974) *Ecstasy and Holiness*. London: Methuen

Newman, F.M. and D.W. Oliver (1967) 'Education and community.' *Harvard Education Review* 37, 1

Nisbet, R.A. (1969) *Social Change and History*. New York: Oxford University Press

NTL (1968) 'What is OD?' *News and Reports*. Washington: NTL Institute. Reprint no. 2, no. 3, June

Osborn, A.F. (1961) *Applied Imagination*. Revised ed. New York: Scribners.

Parsons, T. (1969) *Politics and Social Structure*. New York: Free Press

Pelz, E.B. (1965) 'Some factors in group decision.' In H. Proshansky and B. Seidenberg, eds. *Basic Studies in Social Psychology*. New York: Holt, Rinehart and Winston

Pepper, S.C. (1942) *World Hypotheses*. Berkeley: University of California

Peterson, R.E. (1970) 'The crisis of purpose: definition and use of institutional goals.' Report no. 5, ERIC Clearing House on Higher Education. Princeton: Educational Testing Service

– and W. (1960) *University Adult Education*. New York: Harper and Row

Pirsig, R.M. (1975) *Zen and the Art of Motorcycle Maintenance*. Toronto: Bantam Books

Popham, W.J. and E.L. Baker (1970) *Systematic Instruction*. Englewood Cliffs NJ: Prentice Hall

Powell, J.W. and K. Benne (1960) 'Philosophies of adult education.' In M.S. Knowles, ed. *Handbook of Adult Education in the United States*. Chicago: Adult Education Association of the United States of America

Reich, C. (1970) *The Greening of America*. New York: Bantam Books

Rice, A.K. (1957) *Productivity and Social Organization: The Ahmedabad Experiment*. London: Tavistock

Riley, N.W. (1963) *Sociological Research – A Case Approach*. New York: Harcourt, Brace and World

Roberts, H.W. (1973) 'Comparative studies in lifelong education.' *Journal of the International Congress of University Adult Education* 12, no. 1

Rogers, C. (1969) *Freedom to Learn*. Columbia, Ohio: Merrill

Ross, Murray G. and B.W. Lappin (1967) *Community Organization*. New York: Harper and Row

Roszak, T. (1968) *The Making of a Counter Culture*. New York:
New York: Anchor-Doubleday

Rothman, Jack (1968) 'Three models of community organization practice.' From
National Conference on Social Welfare, *Social Work Practice*. New York:
Columbia University Press

Rubin, I. (1969) 'Function and structure of community: conceptual and theoretical analysis.' *International review of Community Development* no. 21-2

Russell, Bertrand (1971) *Autobiography, 1944-67*. London: George Allen and
Unwin

Sanders, I.T. (1968) *Community Development*. International Encyclopedia of the
Social Sciences, vol. 3. Macmillan/Free Press

Schon, D.A. (1971) *Beyond the Stable State*. New York: Norton

Selznick, P. (1969) 'Foundations of the theory of organization.' In F.E. Emery, ed.
Systems Thinking. Harmondsworth: Penguin

Simey, T.S. (1968) *Social Science and Social Purpose*. London: Constable

Skinner, B.F. (1962) *Walden Two*. New York: Macmillan Paperbacks

– (1971) *Beyond Freedom and Dignity*. New York: Alfred Knopf

Slater, Philip (1970) *The Pursuit of Loneliness*. Boston: Beacon Press

Special Planning Secretariat (1965) 'Community development in Alberta.'
Ottawa: Privy Council Office

Spence, K.W. (1959) 'The relationship of learning theory to the technology of
education.' *Harvard Educational Review*, spring

Sprott, W.J.H. (1958) *Human Groups*. Harmondsworth: Penguin

Srinivasan, L. (1977) *Perspectives on Non-Formal Adult Learning*. New York:
World Education

Stensland, P. (1976) 'The educational core of development.' *Adult Education
(USA)* 26, no. 2

TANU (1967) *The Arusha Declaration and TANU's Policy on Socialism and Self-
Reliance*. Dar es Salaam: TANU Publicity Section

Tawney, R.H. (1938) *Religion and the Rise of Capitalism*. Harmondsworth:
Penguin

Taylor, Carl A. (1956) *A Critical Analysis of India's Community Development
Programme*. Government of India: Ministry of Community Development

Thelen, H. (1954) *Dynamics of Groups at Work*: Chicago: University of Chicago
Press

Thorndike, E.L. and A.I. Gates (1930) *Elementary Principles of Education*. New
York: Macmillan

Trist, E. (1968) 'Urban North America: the challenge of the next thirty years.'
Paper delivered at Town Planning Institute of Canada Conference, Minaki,
Ontario

Upton, A. (1961) *Design for Thinking*. Palo Alto: Stanford University Press

Vaill, P.B. (1967) 'Industrial engineering and socio-technical systems.' *Journal of Industrial Engineering*, Sept.

- (1974) 'The expository model of science in organization design.' Washington, DC: School of Government and Business Administration, George Washington University

Van Den Ven, A. and A.L. Delbecq (1971) 'Nominee versus interacting group processes for committee decision-making effectiveness.' *Academy of Management Journal* no. 14, June

Vanek, J. and T. Bayard (1974-5) 'Education toward self management: an alternative development strategy.' *International Development Review* 17, no. 4

Verner, C. (1971) 'Community action and learning: a concept of analysis.' In J.A. Draper, *Citizen Participation: Canada*. Toronto: New Press

Von Bertalanffy, L. (1969) 'General systems theory – a critical review.' In J.A. Litterer, *Organizations*, vol. 2. New York: Wiley

Wallen, J.L. (1969) *The Interpersonal Gap*. Portland, Ore: Northwest Regional Education Laboratory

Warren, R.L. (1963) *The Community in America*. New York: Rand-McNally

- (1974) 'Community change: some lessons from the recent past.' *Community Development Journal* 9, no. 1

Whyte, W.F. (1943) *Street Corner Society*. Chicago: University of Chicago Press

Wolff, R.P. (1965) 'Beyond tolerance.' In R.P. Wolff, B. Moore, and H. Marcuse, *A Critique of Pure Tolerance*. Boston: Beacon Press

Young, M. and P. Wilmott (1957) *Family and Kinship in East London*. London: Routledge and Kegan Paul

Index